RECREATIONAL
KAYAKING

THE ULTIMATE GUIDE

KEN WHITING

PHOTOS BY JOCK BRADLEY & PAUL VILLECOURT

RECREATIONAL KAYAKING

THE ULTIMATE GUIDE

KEN WHITING

PHOTOS BY JOCK BRADLEY & PAUL VILLECOURT

Published by

 THE **HELICONIA PRESS**

The Heliconia Press, Inc.
1576 Beachburg Road, Beachburg, Ontario K0J 1C0 Canada
www.helipress.com

Written by: Ken Whiting
Edited by: Lori Covington
Photography by: Jock Bradley & Paul Villecourt, except as noted.
Design by: Ken Whiting
Layout by: Robyn Hader

Library and Archives Canada Cataloguing in Publication.

Whiting, Ken, 1974-
      Recreational kayaking : the ultimate guide / Ken
Whiting ; photos by Jock Bradley & Paul Villecourt.

ISBN 978-1-896980-42-3

      1. Kayaking. I. Bradley, Jock, 1961- II. Villecourt, Paul, 1971-
III. Title.

GV783.W54 2009   797.122'4   C2008-906910-2

About Safety
Kayaking is an activity with inherent risks, and this book is designed as a general
guide, not a substitute for experience. The publisher and the author do not take
responsibility for the use of any of the materials or methods described in this book.
By following any of the procedures described within, you do so at your own risk.

To my wife, Nicole, whose unquestioning support and understanding puts a smile on my face each and every day.

TABLE OF CONTENTS

INTRODUCTION

Sometimes, while driving into the city to run errands, I find myself mesmerized by the sheer volume of people. I wonder how many of these people have had the good fortune to be introduced to the sport of kayaking? The truth of the matter is that remarkably few people will ever discover the magic of kayaking. Part of me revels in the fact that I have something unique that means so much to me. At the same time, I earnestly hope that the people around me have found something else that offers the same type of lifelong rewards that kayaking does.

The obvious question that this brings up is why! Why do relatively few people ever discover kayaking? It's not like most people don't have good places to kayak. Name me one village, town or city that doesn't have a significant body of water within 50 miles! The best answer I have been able to come up with has to do with the image that kayaking conjures in the minds of most people.

For many, the word will conjure up images of extreme paddling; a sport of adrenaline junkies charging through raging rapids. Some folks think of it as dangerous, imagining that it's easy to get trapped underwater in a kayak.

The reality is that kayaking is one of the most approachable, straightforward and user-friendly ways to enjoy the outdoors. Personally, I take immense pleasure in dispelling apprehensions about getting into a kayak for the first time because newcomers to the sport routinely discover that kayaking is easy and fun. It truly is a sport for everyone:

kids, teens, adults and seniors; families, couples and individuals. Paddling is a terrific platform for getting outside and spending time with friends and loved ones, but it's also a great way to meet new people, too. Far more interesting than spending time in a gym, paddling can be combined with fishing, bird watching, or simply exploring on your local waterways. Kayaking can be so many different things to so many different types of people that everyone is sure to have a good time.

This book is about recreational kayaking, and it's important to understand from the outset that recreational kayaking is not limited to the use of what are considered to be recreational kayaks. One can go "recreational kayaking" in a specialized boat, such as a sea kayak, whitewater kayak, or racing kayak. The term "recreational kayaking" doesn't necessarily refer to the equipment you use, but the environment in which you paddle. As long as you paddle in a body of water that offers good protection from wind, waves, and whitewater rapids,

and stay close enough to shore that you can always comfortably swim there and get help, then it can be considered recreational kayaking.

Although recreational kayaking is a remarkably safe sport, any activity in a water environment—whether it's swimming, surfing, or boating by wind, motor or paddle—there is always some inherent risk. The fact that you're reading this book means that you're interested in learning more, and it's a great start. Please understand, however, that a book or video is limited in its ability to effectively pass on skills and knowledge; as your confidence grows and you get more into it, consider formal instruction.

Finally, let me congratulate you for being one of the remarkably few people in this world who will step into, and take advantage of, the magical world of kayaking. I'm sure you'll find that on the days you paddle, the world is a little bit brighter.

ABOUT THE AUTHOR

KEN WHITING

Through the 1990s, Ken became one of the most recognized and respected whitewater athletes in the world. Ken was the 1997/98 World Freestyle Kayaking Champion, the 1998 Japan Open Champion, and a five-time National Champion. In 2002, Ken retired from whitewater competition, began exploring all forms of kayaking and focused his passion for paddling on the development of instructional books and DVDs. Ken is now one of the most influential paddlers in the world, and was recognized by *Paddler* magazine as one of their "Paddlers of the Century." He has paddled extensively around the world and has ten best-selling, award-winning instructional books and DVDs to his name. Ken has also co-founded an industry-leading kayak school, and an adventure kayaking travel company with a base camp in Chile's Patagonia region. Ken and his wife Nicole live in Beachburg, Canada, where they run their publishing business, The Heliconia Press. For more information, visit www.helipress.com

JOCK BRADLEY

Whether bushwhacking through Philippine jungles, rappelling into vertical gorges or diving into ocean depths, Jock consistently overcomes tremendous obstacles to obtain the perfect shot. It is, above all, this type of dedication and work ethic that sets him apart—making him one of the world's foremost professional outdoor photographers. For more info, visit www.jockbradley.com.

PAUL VILLECOURT

Paul Villecourt is a French photographer and paddler dedicated to capturing the sensations of adventure and outdoor sports. His passion for paddling has taken him and his camera to all corners of the world. Paul is regarded as one of the finest outdoor photographers in the world, and his work has been featured in virtually every outdoor magazine in Europe and North America. For more info, visit www.villecourt.com.

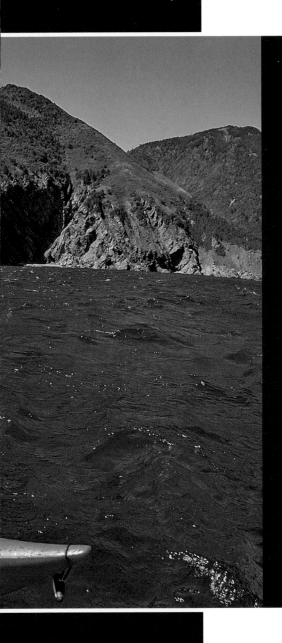

EQUIPMENT

As with any activity, the gear you use for kayaking will have a real impact on how comfortable you are on the water. So while it doesn't necessarily make sense to go out and buy all top of the line gear in the beginning, it is worth investing in decent gear that you can grow with as a paddler. Ultimately, as you gain experience, you'll be able to identify more specifically the type and style of equipment that best suits your paddling style. In this section, we're going to look at the different options that are available and the pros and cons of each, starting with the "big three" pieces of gear—the kayak, the paddle, and the PFD.

THE KAYAK

photo by Edward S. Curtis

Although there are many different forms of kayaking, this book is focused primarily on the very broad category recognized as recreational kayaking. It's important to understand from the outset that recreational kayaking is not limited to the use of what are considered to be recreational kayaks. One can go "recreational kayaking" in a specialized boat, such as a sea kayak, whitewater kayak, or racing kayak. This is because the term "recreational kayaking" doesn't necessarily refer to the equipment you use, but rather the environment in which you paddle. As long as you paddle in a body of water that offers good protection from wind, waves, and whitewater rapids, and stay close enough to shore that you can always comfortably swim there and get help in the event of a capsize, then it can be considered recreational kayaking.

With that said, we're going to look at all the different types of kayaks and identify their advantages and disadvantages with the hopes of helping you make a decision as to which one best fits your needs. There are four different styles of kayaks that we're going to look at. We'll look at recreational kayaks, sea / touring kayaks, whitewater kayaks and racing kayaks. But first, we're going to take a quick look at the history of the kayak.

This Inuit seal hunter uses a traditional Greenland kayak made from seal sinew stretched over a wood frame.

A QUICK HISTORY OF THE KAYAK

The first kayaks were made thousands of years ago by the Inuit—the inhabitants of Greenland, northeastern Russia, Alaska and northern Canada formerly known as Eskimos. Their kayaks were developed primarily as vehicles for hunting and fishing during the summer months, once the ice had broken. In fact, the word kayak literally means "hunter's boat." These early kayaks were made by lashing bone and driftwood together with seal sinew or gut to create a frame. This frame was then wrapped in seal or caribou skin, sewn together, stretched taut and then dried. To waterproof the boats, boiled seal oil or caribou fat was smeared over the seams.

These original kayaks were made in a variety of shapes and sizes to accommodate the differing conditions in which they were being used. For example, a wider, larger kayak provided more storage space for game and supplies and offered more stability in rough seas. On the other hand, longer and narrower kayaks were faster and allowed the paddler to cover more territory.

It wasn't really until 1907 that the kayak was discovered by the rest of the

Since surviving a swim in the freezing cold arctic water wasn't really an option, the Inuit used a special jacket made from seal skin called a *tuilik*, which was laced to the kayak to create a waterproof seal. This helped make the Eskimo roll both possible and necessary. The modern version of the tuilik is the spray skirt that is used by both whitewater and sea kayakers.

world, when a German inventor named Johann Klepper bought a design for a folding kayak from a student and began making kayaks with canvas stretched over a wooden frame. This marked the beginning of the kayak's use for recreational purposes.

Kayaking grew in popularity throughout Europe over the next thirty years and, in the 1930s, folding kayaks started to get used for all types of paddling—including whitewater river running. In 1936, kayak racing became a part of the Olympic Games. During World War II, folding kayaks were even used for secret missions.

In the 1950s, the first fiberglass kayaks were made. The development of plastic, rotomolded kayaks followed in the 1970s. Since then, kayak design has evolved tremendously for numerous specialized purposes, although sea kayaks have maintained fairly close ties to the original kayaks used by the Inuit. In fact, many of the current sea kayak designs show clear influence from the traditional kayaks of Alaska, Canada and Greenland.

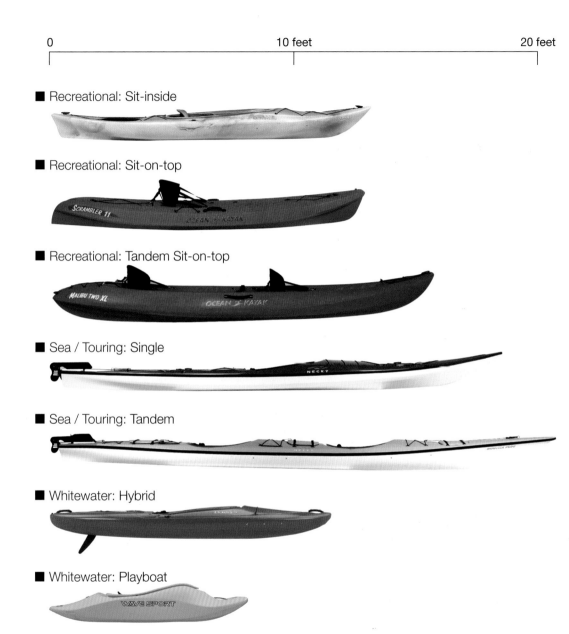

0   10 feet   20 feet

■ Recreational: Sit-inside

■ Recreational: Sit-on-top

■ Recreational: Tandem Sit-on-top

■ Sea / Touring: Single

■ Sea / Touring: Tandem

■ Whitewater: Hybrid

■ Whitewater: Playboat

■ Racing: Single

TYPES OF KAYAKS

[SIZE CHART]

Recreational Kayaks

Recreational kayaks represent the largest number of kayaks on the market and come in a wide range of shapes and sizes. They are designed to be stable, fun and easy to use and range from ten to fifteen feet in length. They are ideal for people willing to give up some boat performance in order to minimize their chances of capsizing, and to maximize their comfort.

Rec boats come in two basic styles, "sit-on-top" and "sit-inside," and both are available as singles (for one person) or tandems (for two). They're also available in hard shell, folding or inflatable materials. Hard shell, plastic kayaks are generally the most popular because they require no set-up and are extremely durable. But inflatable and folding kayaks are really handy if you don't have the storage space or the means to transport a full-sized kayak, because they can be rolled into a backpack-sized bag.

Sea / Touring Kayaks

Sea kayaks, otherwise referred to as touring kayaks, are sit-inside kayaks designed to travel quickly in variable conditions, although they do so at the sacrifice of some stability. Sea kayaks are longer than recreational kayaks (between fourteen and nineteen feet long), and they have smaller cockpits that allow for outfitting features like thigh hooks, which offer the paddler much better boat control and make rolling a kayak possible. They have built-in flotation created by bulkheads which divide the boat's interior into separate watertight compartments. These compartments are accessed through hatches on the deck. Not only do these compartments offer relatively dry spots for carrying gear for day or camping trips, but they also provide valuable flotation in case the boat capsizes. Sea or touring kayaks will also have either a rudder or skeg which is used to help the kayak go straight.

Sea kayaks are available as both singles or doubles. Although folding sea kayaks aren't uncommon for those lacking the ability to deal with a full-sized kayak, most sea kayaks are hard shells, made of plastic or composite materials.

Whitewater Kayaks

Whitewater kayaks are the shortest of the kayak family (between six and twelve feet in length). They are designed for maneuverability as much as for speed, which means they turn quickly but they don't travel well in a straight line. Most whitewater kayaks are not suited for flat-water paddling for this reason, although there are some new recreational / whitewater hybrid kayaks that are now available which are suitable for flat-water paddlers who also enjoy paddling in light river current. These hybrid kayaks are longer than regular whitewater kayaks and they come with a rudder to help one travel in straight line on flat-water. These are great boats if you will be paddling in rivers with moving water.

All whitewater kayaks are hard shells made of durable and affordable polyethylene (plastic).

Racing Kayaks

Racing kayaks are designed to go as fast as possible on flat, calm, protected waters only, which make them a lot of fun to paddle. They are between sixteen and twenty-two feet long, are made of the lightest materials and have hull shapes designed for speed, not stability. Although there are fairly stable beginner models available, they are still not generally suitable for new paddlers. Sprint kayaks are the fastest racing kayaks, but there are also multisport racing kayaks which deal better with rougher conditions.

Racing kayaks are just wide enough for your hips, which makes them super fast, but unstable.

Kayaks can be manufactured from a wide variety of materials, but fall within three structural classes: hard shell, folding and inflatable.

Hard shell kayaks are the most popular kayaks and what most people picture when they think of a kayak. Hard shells are constructed of plastic, composite materials (fiberglass, Kevlar, and carbon fiber), or wood. The most common material used to make kayaks is a durable polyethylene (a type of plastic) because it is very affordable and has amazing durability. Composite kayaks are lighter and more attractive, but they're also twice the price.

Folding kayaks are collapsible boats made of fabric stretched over either a wood or aluminum frame. Most folding kayaks will fit into a backpack-sized bag when taken apart. Folding kayaks are expensive but they paddle well and are very convenient if you don't have the storage space, or the means to transport a full-sized kayak.

Inflatable kayaks are made from coated fabrics and, like folding kayaks, they pack down into a backpack-sized bag. Inflatable kayaks are affordable, durable, and convenient if you can't handle a full-sized kayak, but they lack the performance of a folding or hard shell kayak.

PARTS OF THE KAYAK

Although the above-mentioned kayaks vary a great deal, they share many of the same parts. The top of a kayak is referred to as the deck. The bottom is the hull. The front of the boat is called the bow, and the back is the stern. On deck, you'll often find deck lines that make it really easy to grab the boat, and bungee cords that you can use to secure extra equipment like water bottles or sunscreen. You'll also find convenient carrying handles at both the bow and stern.

Some boats have a rudder or skeg to help keep the boat running straight (although neither are essential pieces of equipment). Rudders offer much more control as they swivel from side to side and are controlled by foot pedals. Skegs are fixed along the centerline on the bottom of the boat and can be lowered to help the boat go straight in windy conditions.

All kayaks have some form of seat and support for the feet, such as foot pedals or foot wells. They should also have some type of lower back support, like a back band or a seat back.

Unique to sit-inside kayaks is the cockpit—the area within the boat where you sit. Around the cockpit you'll find the cockpit rim, otherwise referred to as the coaming. This raised lip allows a sprayskirt to be attached to the boat in order to keep water out.

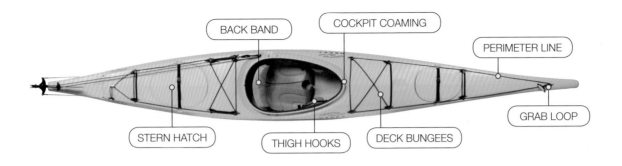

BACK BAND · COCKPIT COAMING · PERIMETER LINE · STERN HATCH · THIGH HOOKS · DECK BUNGEES · GRAB LOOP

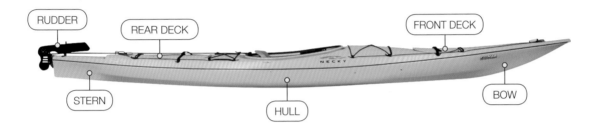

RUDDER · REAR DECK · FRONT DECK · STERN · HULL · BOW

CHOOSING THE RIGHT KAYAK

As you can see, kayaks come in all sorts of shapes and sizes, so it's easy to get a little overwhelmed when trying to decide which kayak is best for you. Take heart, though, because the decision does not need to be a difficult one. The best way to narrow down your options is by clearly identifying how and where you'll be using your kayak, and then determining your budget for the purchase.

Your first and biggest decision is whether to go for a sit-on-top or a sit-inside kayak, and there are pros and cons to

both. Sit-on-tops provide the ultimate in user-friendliness. Since you sit right on top of the kayak, your legs are totally free (although you can opt to use thigh straps that allow you to grip the kayak with your legs) and there is no feeling of confinement that sometimes accompanies a sit-inside. Sit-on-tops are also self-bailing, meaning that water automatically drains out of the seat and foot wells through scupper holes that go right through the kayak. Their inherent stability also makes them very safe and fun to use. In fact, I often call

In order to choose the right kayak, you first need to identify how and where you'll be using it. For example, a sit-on-top is great for fishing because you can sit sideways on it.

them floating docks because you can just slip on and off them while you're on the water. If you do somehow flip the kayak, they don't even require emptying out—just flip them upright and scramble aboard! All these features make sit-on-top kayaks great for more nervous paddlers, for paddling in warm environments, and for paddling in places where flipping is a more distinct possibility.

Although these are some pretty compelling reasons to choose a sit-on-top kayak, there are also some great reasons to choose a sit-inside kayak. In fact, one of the sit-on-top's strengths is also its greatest weakness: the fact that you're not enclosed means that you'll almost always get wet. On the other hand, sit-inside kayaks allow you to stay much drier and they protect your lower body from the wind. The option of using a spray deck further increases a paddler's defenses against cold and wetness. For this reason, sit-inside kayaks are very popular in areas where both warm water and hot air temperatures aren't the norm. Like sit-on-tops, recreational sit-inside kayaks are generally very stable and easy to use. They also have large cockpits that minimize any possible feelings of confinement, and offer easy entry and exit from the boat. The downside of the sit-inside kayaks is that you don't have the same freedom to hop in and out of them while on the water and, more importantly, recovering from capsizing is not a simple process. Because sit-inside kayaks are not self-bailing, if you capsize,

your boat will swamp, which is a bit of a pain to deal with. Sea kayaks (and some sit-inside rec kayaks) have built-in flotation created by bulkheads, which are waterproof walls on the inside of the kayak that divide the boat's interior into separate compartments. These compartments are accessed through hatches on the deck, and not only do they generate valuable flotation in case you capsize, but they also provide a relatively dry spot for carrying gear.

Once you have decided on whether to go for a sit-on-top or sit-inside kayak, you've already narrowed your options considerably. Here are some of the next issues to consider.

Stability vs Speed

As a general rule, the longer and narrower a boat is, the faster it will be. However, the wider a boat is the more stable it will become. If you are willing to give up some stability for the sake of speed, you're probably a good candidate for a sea /touring kayak, or even a racing kayak if you're really interested in flying and aren't concerned about flipping. Another factor that influences stability versus speed is the shape of the kayak's hull. There are three main hull shapes to consider: flat, rounded, and V-shaped.

Flat hulls make for the most stable kayaks, but also the slowest.

Rounded hulls are faster, but less stable than flat hulls.

V-hulls offer a compromise between flat and rounded hulls. Their downside is that they are slightly less maneuverable.

Maneuverability vs Speed

Another general rule about kayaks is that shorter boats will turn much more easily than longer boats, which track in a straight line and travel more quickly. So, if you plan on going on long paddles, you'll probably want a long rec kayak, or sea kayak. If you plan on fooling around on a small lake or paddling on a river with obstacles, you'll want a shorter and more maneuverable kayak.

Transportation

Your ability to both carry and drive with a kayak will have a real impact on the type of kayak you should get. Obviously, a shorter and lighter kayak will be easier to carry and will make transportation less cumbersome as well. On the other hand, if your kayak is going to live at the cottage, or you're just a strong person who isn't worried about carrying a longer boat, then perhaps this isn't a real issue. If you don't have the means to transport, or the space to store a full-sized kayak, consider a folding or inflatable kayak. Folding kayaks are generally faster but less stable than inflatable kayaks.

V-HULL   FLAT HULL   ROUNDED HULL

V-hulls provide exceptional tracking, flat hulls provide superior stability, and rounded hulls are good for speed and holding on edge.

Durability

The most durable kayaks on the market are those made of plastic, or high quality inflatables. Both will take a remarkable amount of abuse. Not surprisingly, these are great options if you don't like to have to worry about maintaining your equipment, or if there are kids or dogs in the picture. Of course, if you don't mind taking care of your gear, or paying more for a higher performance kayak, then a folding or composite kayak might make sense.

Cost

Cost can play a big role in your ultimate decision, as similar types of kayaks made from different materials can vary in price from $800 to $4000. In general, what you get for the extra money is a lighter, higher performance boat that usually has a few extra bells and whistles, which may or may not be of concern to you. If you're willing to spend the cash and are looking for a higher performance boat, a composite sea kayak or folding kayak is a great option. If you're looking for an affordable, durable, but slightly heavier kayak, an inflatable or plastic kayak is your best option.

If you expect to drag your kayak around, your only good option is a plastic kayak.

Canoes and kayaks are both amazing watercraft with devoted followers and huge historical importance within North America. That being said, both have their pros and cons, which we're now going to look at. If you're currently trying to decide between a kayak and a canoe, hopefully this will help you. More likely though, I expect that this will convince you that you need at least one of each!

CANOE VS KAYAK

THE GREAT DEBATE

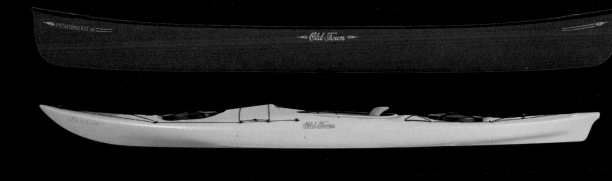

Advantages of a Canoe

1. Great for camping trips
    a. They carry a huge amount of gear
    b. Easy to portage
2. Paddlers tend to stay drier
3. Freedom to change leg positions
4. Easier to get into and out of

Advantages of a Kayak

1. Easier to control in windy conditions
2. Much more stable in rough conditions
3. Waterproof storage compartments keep gear contained and relatively dry in case of a capsize
4. Travels faster
5. Easier to paddle solo
6. Easier to reenter from the water

Both are:

1. Great with kids and dogs
2. Great cottage boats
3. Great tandem boats
4. A pleasure to paddle

THE PADDLE

While it's true that almost any paddle will probably do the trick, there are a lot of great reasons to take the time to choose the right paddle for what you want to do.

For casual paddling, almost any paddle durable enough to stand up to the abuse it's bound to receive, and that will effectively propel your kayak forward, is perfectly adequate. Of course, a good quality paddle does have real benefits. It will make your time on the water more comfortable, more enjoyable, and more efficient.

Paddles have three main parts. They have a shaft, a power face, and a back face. The power face is the side of the paddle blade that catches water when you take a forward stroke, while the back face, of course, is the other side of the blade. From tip to tip, paddles can vary in length from 180 centimeters to 260 centimeters (rarely measured in inches). Blades also come in a wide range of shapes and sizes.

Bent-shaft paddles are more and more commonly seen. The idea behind the bent shaft is that it puts your hand and wrist in a more natural position while you paddle, which reduces strain on your wrist. There's an ongoing debate about how effective bent-shafts really are, so you'll want to try one yourself and make up your own mind.

CHOOSING A PADDLE

When choosing a paddle, the two most important factors that you'll need to consider are its length and blade size. Your physical size and the width of your kayak will play the largest roles making this decision. As a general rule, a smaller paddler should use smaller blades, while a stronger paddler can control a paddle with larger blades. Similarly, it will be easier to use a longer paddle for a wider kayak, while shorter paddles are more appropriate for narrower kayaks. Taller people will also generally need longer paddles. The type of paddling that you plan to do will play an equally important role in your paddle decision. Shorter paddles promote a more vertical, and

therefore more aggressive stroke. Longer paddles make a lower-angle stroke more comfortable; a more relaxing style better suited for casual or longer distance paddling.

As for the size of your blades, long, skinny blades, with fairly small surface areas, are the best choice for casual or long distance paddling. These paddles will often have a soft, dihedral shape to their power face, which means the two faces of the blade on either side of the center line slope away slightly. This causes the paddle to catch less water, which allows for a smoother and less energy-consuming stroke. For more aggressive

A Rough Guide to Paddle Length

A TYPE OF KAYAK	PERSONAL HEIGHT	
	5'4"	6'
Rec (sit-inside)	230cm	240cm
Rec (sit-on-top)	240cm	250cm
Sea kayak	220cm	230cm
Whitewater kayak	190cm	200cm
Racing kayak	210cm	220cm

paddling you'll want to use a wider blade, with more of a 'cupped' shape, because it catches more water and provides more power with each stroke. Racing paddles, otherwise known as wing paddles, take this to the extreme, with an ultra-aggressive power face designed to catch a maximum amount of water.

A final decision you'll need to make has to do with the feather, or offset, of your blades. The feather is the amount of twist between the blades of a paddle. The advantage of having offset blades is that in a headwind, the top blade slices through the air with minimal air resistance, while the bottom blade is pulled through the water. On the other hand, a paddle with no offset is much more intuitive, less likely to cause tendonitis (because your wrists don't need to perform the same repetitive twisting motion), and in my opinion the best option for most paddlers. One nice thing is that most recreational kayaking paddles come as two-piece designs and provide the option of being assembled with or without offset blades. There is no right way here; just personal preference.

Some paddles come with drip rings, which are rubber rings that stop drips from your blades from reaching your hands. The drip rings should be positioned close to the blades, although not so close that they get submerged while paddling.

Did You Know?

Did You Know?

A good way to test whether or not a life jacket fits right is to put it on and tighten it as you would to wear it on the water. Then, hook your thumbs under the shoulder straps and tug upward. The life jacket should stay in place around your body and not ride up around your ears. If it's riding up more than a little, try a smaller life jacket.

THE LIFE JACKET / PFD

Your life jacket, or PFD (Personal Flotation Device), is your single most important piece of safety equipment, but of course it's only helpful if you're wearing it correctly. If you're not wearing it properly, or it doesn't fit right, a PFD can actually impede your ability to swim. In order for a PFD to fit right, it should have a number of cinch straps on the sides and at the waist so that it can be tightened to fit like a pair of shoes: snug but comfortable.

Any Coast Guard–approved PFD that fits well and is comfortable enough that you won't feel the need to remove it while on the water is perfectly adequate. With that said, the best PFDs for kayaking are the ones specifically designed for that purpose. Kayaking PFDs have large armholes, and their flotation is positioned away from the shoulders and upper chest, so your arms have the fullest range of motion. Many life jackets also have convenient features such as zippered pockets for carrying things like sunscreen, glasses and snacks. Some models even have pouches for hydration bladders that can be mounted on the back of the PFD.

A paddling-specific life jacket has large armholes and keeps the flotation away from the shoulders to offer you the fullest range of motion.

Drying the gear and ourselves after a day's paddle in Maine.

CLOTHING

Dressing for paddling can be very simple, or quite complex. When making the decision, you need to consider the worst-case scenario (capsizing at the furthest point from home) and then look at four major factors: the temperature of the air, the temperature of the water, the longest time you could spend in the water, and the longest you could spend paddling home wet.

It's also worth noting that the type of boat you're using will impact how you'll need to dress. If you're paddling a sit-on-top kayak, you should expect your lower body to get wet, whereas a sit-inside will provide far more protection from wind and water.

Dressing for warm conditions primarily involves protecting yourself from the sun.

DRESSING FOR WARM CONDITIONS

When the air and water is warm, dressing for kayaking isn't very hard. The biggest challenges you'll usually face are staying cool, hydrated and protected from the sun. Of course, that's where sunscreen, a hat, and sunglasses (with a retainer strap, or tied to your lifejacket so you don't lose them) come in. Otherwise, a light shirt, quick-drying shorts and sandals work well. Even though you may never need it, it's not a bad idea to throw a warmer piece of gear, like a windbreaker, into your boat. A brisk wind at the end of the day can cool you down very quickly.

DRESSING FOR COLD WATER

If you're paddling in cold water when the air is warm, dressing appropriately is a bit more complicated. Cold water can suck the heat out of your body fast and quickly lead to hypothermia. On the flip side, being overdressed and paddling in hot weather can result in dangerous overheating. You need to find a happy medium, and keep in mind that as long as you bring some extra pieces of clothing, you can always layer up after a capsize.

A paddling top with latex gaskets at the wrists will stop cold water from running down your forearms and pooling in the sleeves of your jacket, where it likes to wait for you to lift your arms so that it can run down your sides and send shock waves up your spine.

DRESSING FOR COLD CONDITIONS

When both the air and the water are cold, you've got to protect yourself from the possibility of hypothermia. Not only does this mean dressing appropriately, but it means choosing a paddling route that never takes you too far from somewhere you can go to warm up. Of course, the best strategy for staying warm is to avoid capsizing altogether, which means sticking to bodies of water that are protected from wind and waves. With that said, you still need to dress with the assumption that you'll capsize at the furthest point away from a warm, dry location.

When it comes to dressing, follow the layering guidelines, and bring extra gear (stored in a dry bag) in case the gear you're using gets wet. You'll also want to consider wearing something to keep your head and hands warm. A warm hat and neoprene gloves or pogies work great in most situations. Pogies are gloves that attach to your paddle so you can slip your hands inside and have direct contact with your paddle shaft.

LAYERING FOR WARMTH

A layered clothing system is best for any activity, paddling included. Your first layer, the base layer, should be a wicking layer—designed to draw moisture away from your body. This is where synthetic materials like polypropylene and Capilene are great—and where cotton is terrible! Another option for paddling is a neoprene wetsuit. In particular, the armless Farmer John/Jane style is good for paddling. Neoprene is specifically designed to insulate your body when it's wet.

The next layer should be an insulating layer, made from a material that insulates whether it's wet or dry. Ideally, the insulating layer should fit closely, without restricting your movement. Wool works well, although it gets really heavy and cumbersome when it's wet. Fleece is an ideal insulating layer, and it's available in all sorts of thicknesses to accommodate different conditions.

The outer layer should protect you from wind and water. Waterproof nylon jackets and pants work well, although the best outer layers are paddling-specific jackets and pants made from materials like Gore-Tex—waterproof and breathable. Paddling-specific jackets are designed to accommodate your life jacket and other accessories like a spray skirt. They also give lots of room in the shoulders, so your arms have maximum freedom of movement.

The ultimate protection against the cold is a dry suit. A dry suit has latex gaskets at the ankles, wrists and neck to keep all water out, even when you're completely immersed. Dry suits are expensive, but if you spend a lot of time paddling in cold conditions they're a great investment in both comfort and safety.

FOOTWEAR

The appropriate footwear is dictated by the paddling environment and the air and water temperature. If you're paddling in a warm environment, you'll want to choose footwear that allows your feet to breathe, such as sandals or water shoes. If you need to walk on rocks or other uneven terrain, you'll probably want to go for a water shoe, as they offer more foot protection and better overall support.

If you're paddling in cold water, or both cold water and air, you'll want something warmer on your feet. One option is to just throw on a pair of wool or neoprene

socks under your sandals or water shoes, but the better option is to use a neoprene shoe (often called booties). Just like a wetsuit, a neoprene bootie is designed to insulate when it's wet. If your feet are really susceptible to the cold, you can even wear a pair of neoprene or wool

socks inside your neoprene booties. Some booties have thick, hard soles for walking on rough terrain, while others have relatively soft and flexible soles that give you better contact with the foot pegs of your kayak, and which fit more comfortably in narrow sit-inside kayaks.

Water shoes provide more protection and support than sandals and are designed to drain and dry quickly.

ACCESSORIES

SPRAY SKIRT

If you're paddling a sit-inside kayak, you can wear a spray skirt, also known as a spray deck, which wraps around the coaming of your cockpit and keeps water out. Spray skirts all have rip cords that allow you to pop the skirt off the boat when you need to get out. The part of the skirt that covers the cockpit of your kayak is called the deck, and the part that wraps around your waist is called the tunnel.

Spray skirts are nice additions when you're paddling in cold water, or in windy or rough conditions. All sea kayakers and whitewater kayakers wear spray skirts to allow their kayaks to deal with rough water conditions and to let them roll their kayaks upright if they capsize. Since recreational kayakers avoid rough conditions, and since recreational kayaks don't usually have the necessary outfitting to allow the paddler to roll it upright, there's much less reason to wear

a spray skirt. The best reason for a rec kayaker to wear a spray skirt is to keep cold water from dripping on your legs, to warm up the interior of your kayak, and to protect your legs from the sun.

Spray skirts are usually made out of one of two materials; nylon or neoprene. Nylon ones typically are easier to get on and to take off; they cost less, and they breathe more. Neoprene skirts provide the most secure seal on a kayak and keep water out the most effectively, but they're more expensive and harder to get on and off your boat. There are also hybrid skirts with a neoprene deck that creates a nice seal on the kayak, and a nylon waist that's cooler and more comfortable to wear.

Nylon skirts are usually the best choice for recreational paddlers. Sea kayakers should consider a neoprene or hybrid skirt. Whitewater kayakers will use a neoprene skirt.

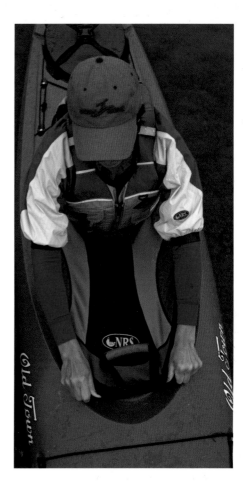

If you are going to get a spray skirt, it's important to know that they aren't one-size-fits-all. You need to get a skirt specifically sized to your boat's coaming.

DRY BAGS / CASES

Dry bags and cases are designed to keep things dry inside, even if they're immersed in water for a long period. Of course, some do a better job than others, and it's fair to say that you get what you pay for. Simple, fold-down dry bags are durable, affordable and do a reasonably good job of keeping things dry, but I wouldn't put anything in them that can't handle a little moisture. Waterproof cases made of high-impact-resistant plastic and sealed with a rubber O-ring (such as Pelican cases) offer the greatest all-around protection, and are particularly good for things like cameras. For carrying things like my wallet, first aid kit, and my little digital camera, I've been using a Watershed dry bag, which uses a Ziploc-style closure system, for the past decade,. Although they're more expensive than normal fold-down dry bags, they are very tough and extremely reliable.

SEATS

Most sit-inside kayaks come with some form of seat that's ready to use. If it isn't padded, you can always glue some foam down to make it a bit more comfortable. Sit-on-top kayaks often don't come with anything more than a contoured seat pan to sit on. Although you can use them as-is, I would highly recommend investing in an adjustable, padded seat. There are some great seats available that will make your time spent on the water much more comfortable. Some of them even have added features like pockets, or even fishing rod holders.

A good seat will make your time on the water much more enjoyable.

SAFETY EQUIPMENT

Kayaking is inherently a very safe sport, and with a conservative attitude and a little common sense, you can avoid almost any hazardous situation. But you still need to prepare yourself for the worst, because sometimes things just happen!

If you stay within the realm of recreational kayaking (which you should know by now means staying close to shore, in areas that are protected from wind and waves, and within reach of a helping hand), you won't need much in the way of safety equipment beyond your PFD. However, it's always a good idea to bring a whistle, sun protection, water and a snack.

As soon as you stray into more exposed conditions, such as paddling in fast-moving current or on an open body of water that doesn't provide protection from wind and waves, the list of safety equipment you need grows very quickly, and in most cases you'll need to be trained in how to use the gear. If you're going down this road, you really need to take an appropriate instructional course. We take a quick look at the safety issues and the equipment that you need to consider in the "Exposed Water Paddling" and "River Running" chapters of this book.

In most areas, it is standard to use a single long blast on the whistle to draw attention to yourself. If you have a serious emergency that needs immediate attention—and only then—three short blasts should be used.

Did You Know?

CHAPTER TWO

BEFORE HITTING THE WATER

CARING FOR YOUR KAYAK

PADDLING POSTURE

OUTFITTING YOUR KAYAK

TRANSPORTING YOUR KAYAK

LIFTING AND CARRYING YOUR KAYAK

WARMING UP AND STRETCHING

PADDLING SAFETY AND COMMON SENSE

CARING FOR YOUR KAYAK

The amount of care and maintenance your kayak needs is very much dependent on the material your kayak is made of. In general though, kayaks are remarkably durable machines, and since they have very few moving parts, there really aren't many things that can go wrong with them. Most damage is the result of the corrosive effects of saltwater, or improper transportation and storage.

To protect your kayak from saltwater, it's worth giving it a quick hose down with freshwater when you're done with it, paying special attention to the moving parts, like the rudders and foot pegs.

We'll be looking at the proper way to transport a kayak in a moment, but here are a couple of things to consider when storing your kayak. First of all,

it's important that you appreciate the damage that prolonged exposure to sun can cause your kayak. Ideally, your kayak should be stored in a cool, dry, sheltered place. If you're leaving it outside, it should be stored upside down or at least leaning far enough on its side so that water won't get into it. Simply put, when off the water, a dry boat is a happy boat.

MAINTAINING A PLASTIC KAYAK

As we discussed earlier, one of the benefits of plastic kayaks is that they are incredibly durable. This is why almost every whitewater kayak is made from polyethylene plastic. You can hit these boats on rocks without really having to worry about doing any significant damage to them. You might scrape or even dent the plastic, but for the most part, this kind of damage will not affect the integrity of your boat, and it can usually be repaired very easily. Scratches in your hull sometimes leave strings of plastic hanging. They can be shaved off with a razor blade and forgotten about, unless the scratch is so deep that it almost punctures the hull. Dents will often pop out on their own, as the plastic has a "memory" and will want to return to its original shape, especially when it's warmed up. Leaving the dent exposed to the sun on a hot summer day will often be enough to pop it out, although you may also need to coax it a little with the palm of your hand.

One of the few downsides of plastic boats is that they tend to deform a bit over time. You could say that their memory gets a little fuzzy. Most commonly, the hull of the kayak will warp, which is often called "oil canning." For the most part, oil canning won't have a noticeable effect on the kayak's performance, unless it's severe. You can often pop the kayak back into shape by leaving it out in the sun, the same way you deal with dents.

MAINTAINING A COMPOSITE KAYAK

Composite kayaks are surprisingly durable, although with a hard enough impact they can crack. Fortunately, cracks in composite kayaks can usually be fixed by someone experienced in that type of work. To keep composite kayaks looking nice, they can be cleaned with a mild detergent and a soft cloth. You might also want to use a car or boat wax on the exterior for added protection against the sun.

MAINTAINING A FOLDING OR INFLATABLE KAYAK

The key to keeping a folding or inflatable kayak in good shape is to store it out of the sun, and keep it as dry as possible, which usually means toweling it off before packing it away. Although both folding and inflatable kayaks are designed to be very durable, it is possible to puncture them. Because so many different materials can be used for these types of boats, most manufacturers will supply a small repair kit, along with instructions on how to use it.

PADDLING POSTURE

In this section, we're going to take a quick look at the ideal sitting position for paddling a kayak because it will impact how comfortable and efficient you are while paddling, and it will help you avoid issues like back pain.

The ideal sitting position in a kayak is comfortably upright, just like the way your mom always told you to sit at the dinner table! Your feet should be resting comfortably and securely against their supports and your legs should be comfortably flexed and somewhat splayed out. Keeping your knees slightly bent will make sitting upright easier and reduce the strain on your hamstrings and back. The higher performance sit-inside kayaks will have thigh hooks, under which your legs will fit. Most kayaks now come with some type of back support, which will help encourage your upright sitting position.

One of the most common reasons for discomfort in a kayak is tight hamstrings, which make it difficult to sit up straight with your legs out in front of you. The most common symptoms of tight hamstrings are leg cramps and lower back pain. Obviously, regular stretching is the best way to deal with this issue, but there are a few quick fixes you can make to your kayak's outfitting to help out—and this is what the next section deals with.

Although there's nothing wrong with lounging in your kayak, when paddling you should sit upright.

OUTFITTING YOUR KAYAK

The outfitting of your kayak refers to the connection between your body and the boat, and it has a large impact on both your control and your comfort in your boat. Fortunately for all of us, kayak outfitting has improved dramatically over the past decade to offer us a more comfortable paddling experience. In some cases your kayak will come with outfitting good enough so you can simply hop on and start paddling. In most cases though, you'll benefit from a little customizing. Often this will mean making simple adjustments to the outfitting that comes with your kayak, but in some cases, particularly for higher performance paddling, you'll want to customize your kayak a bit more. When considering the outfitting of your kayak, you need to look at the support provided to your feet, legs, butt, hips, and lower back.

Good outfitting is all about supporting your legs and making it comfortable to sit upright.

FOOT SUPPORTS

Foot wells easily accommodate paddlers of differing heights.

Foot support is important because it plays a major role in allowing you to comfortably maintain good posture while paddling. Without it, you'll slowly slide down into the seat like you might slide down into a couch while watching a movie. Although I'll be the first one to admit that there's a time and place for that type of lounging, it's not when you're paddling. Ideally, the balls of your feet will be braced against the foot supports, which keep your legs in a comfortably flexed position. Depending on the model of your kayak, it will have foot pegs, foot wells, or a bulkhead system.

Foot pegs are small plates that slide forward and backward along a track to accommodate different leg lengths. These are the most common and easily adjusted form of foot support, and in most cases, the best option, although sand has a tendency to get caught in the track, making their adjustment more difficult over time.

Foot wells are recesses that are molded right into some sit-on-top kayaks; you'll simply place your foot in the most appropriate well for your leg length. Foot wells are convenient but they support the heel of your foot instead of the ball of your foot. This means they offer less control and they don't offer your ankles any support, which makes a difference if you're paddling any distance.

A bulkhead is a system used in a relatively low number of sit-inside kayaks. The bulkhead is an interior wall that slides forward and backward and then gets locked into place. Bulkheads are commonly used in whitewater kayaks for safety reasons (which are only relevant to whitewater kayakers) but they add a significant amount of weight to a kayak, so they're seldom used in any other type of kayak.

LEG SUPPORTS

The leg support your kayak offers partly depends on whether you're using a sit-inside or sit-on-top kayak. Believe it or not, recreational sit-inside kayaks are usually the most comfortable boats out there because they can offer a lot of leg support, while at the same time being big enough to allow you to really stretch out.

As we discussed in the previous segment about sitting in a kayak, the ideal position for your legs is comfortably flexed and somewhat splayed out. You'll have to adjust the position of your foot supports to establish this position. The problem with sit-on-tops is that there is no support for your upper leg or knee. This means that your legs will usually hang freely outward, which over time will cause discomfort in your hips. If you're using a sit-inside, your leg will usually rest against the side of the kayak. If it doesn't, you can glue foam to the inside wall of the kayak so that your leg does rest against it. Higher performance sit-inside kayaks usually have thigh hooks as well, which your legs fit under. Although thigh hooks don't tend to make a boat more comfortable, they offer the single biggest boost in terms of boat control, which is why all sea and whitewater kayaks have them.

A final means of supporting your legs and making paddling more comfortable is to add support under your upper thigh. Many of the better adjustable seats have an adjustment strap that lets you lift the front edge of the seat to support your upper leg. If that isn't an option, you can glue some foam on the part of the seat where your thighs will rest.

A good seat makes a huge difference regarding your comfort.

Did You Know?

Using thigh straps on a sit-on-top kayak is a great way to improve the amount of boat control that you have, although it won't impact your comfort while paddling.

BUTT SUPPORT

There's no doubt that your butt is one of the most padded parts of your body, but that doesn't mean that it won't appreciate a little tender loving care. Many seats now come with seat padding, but if yours doesn't, then it's worth gluing a quarter inch of mini-cell foam onto your boat's seat.

BACK SUPPORT

Back support is absolutely critical for both comfort and performance. There are two choices. You can use a simple back band or a complete seat with full back support. Either way, your back should be supported above the hips, enough to encourage an upright sitting position.

HIP SUPPORT

For recreational paddling, hip support isn't really relevant. On the other hand, for high performance paddling in sit-inside kayaks, hip support is critical in order to be able to aggressively edge your kayak and for advanced techniques like rolling. To add hip support, use foam hip pads in your kayak. Hip padding should be snug enough to prevent your butt's sliding from side to side, but no tighter. It's also very helpful if your hip pads cup slightly over your hips and upper thighs because the pads help keep your butt from falling out of the seat when you're upside down. Of course, you need to be sure that your hip support still allows an easy escape from the kayak.

A good, high-backed seat will really make your time on the water more comfortable.

The ideal roof racks for transporting kayaks are specifically designed for the purpose.

TRANSPORTING YOUR KAYAK

It doesn't take a rocket scientist to realize that strapping a kayak to the roof of a car can be a real recipe for disaster. In fact, most serious damage to kayaks is incurred during transportation, not while in use on the water.

You have three real options when it comes to transporting a kayak. You can tie the kayak onto a roof rack, throw it into the back of a pickup, or tow it in a trailer. If you're going to throw your kayak into the bed of your pickup, make sure it's tied in well and don't forget that in many areas you're required to put a red flag on anything that sticks out very far from the back of your truck. If you're regularly carrying a bunch of kayaks, a trailer is a great option, although there are obvious downsides to using a trailer.

Tying kayaks to the roof rack of a vehicle is the most common way of getting them around. There are a number of roof rack options out there. Unfortunately, factory-installed roof racks usually won't do the trick. They're simply not designed to take a load like a kayak. In fact, they're not really designed to take any type of a real load. The cheapest solution is to use foam blocks on the roof of your vehicle. You'll

A SCARY LESSON

I once thoroughly tested the durability of a composite kayak when a group of us were returning from a sea kayaking trip to Canada's Cape Breton Island. We were driving home with four kayaks strapped to the roof of the camper on my pickup. A car pulled up alongside us on the highway and the driver started waving frantically at me. I quickly understood that we had boat issues and immediately started to slow down. Unfortunately, this all took place moments before passing through an underpass. As we slowed down and traveled through the underpass, we heard a loud bang from above, which nearly caused the lot of us to jump out of our skins. As quickly as possible we pulled over and stopped. What we discovered was that, eleven feet up on the top of the camper, the straps that held the kayaks down on the forward rack had snapped. With the back ends of the kayaks tied securely, the wind had lifted the front ends into the air—like a bear rearing on its hind legs. The ends of the kayaks must have been sixteen to eighteen feet up in the air as we traveled through the underpass. Fortunately, my composite kayak was the longest—and the only kayak that stuck up high enough to catch the bridge. It immediately snapped the end off the kayak, but remarkably caused no further damage. Everyone in our group knew that we had narrowly avoided a real catastrophe. Needless to say, we doubled up all the front straps from that point on, and checked and rechecked those straps regularly. You'll probably be surprised to hear that a few weeks later, my kayak was as good as new—and that's the joy of composite kayaks. They can almost always be repaired.

then strap the kayak down with cam straps that pass through your vehicle. Of course, you'll need to pass the straps through open doors, so you don't end up tying your doors closed. Use straps or ropes to tie lines from your bow and stern to the ends of your vehicle to prevent the kayak(s) from moving forward and backward.

Although foam racks will usually do the trick for short jaunts and low speeds, a much more reliable option is to get real roof racks, such as those that Thule and Yakima make. These guys have developed racks for almost every type of vehicle, along with rack systems designed specifically for transporting kayaks. They have kayak stackers, which make it much easier to carry multiple kayaks, as well as kayak cradles that fit on the racks and hold your boat firmly in place, while protecting the hull. They have rollers which let you load long kayaks more easily. You simply lift one end onto the rollers and then grab the other end and roll the boat onto the racks. They even have some crazy new systems that let you load the kayak onto a low, hanging platform alongside your vehicle, which then easily lifts up and locks into place on top of your vehicle. If you're going to use straight bar racks alone, it's a good idea to pad the racks with foam, and not to leave your kayak on the rack for longer than necessary because over time it will cause warping.

Although loading a kayak onto the roof of a vehicle can be done by one strong person (especially if you have rollers on your rack), it's always easier if you have one person lifting at each end.

To tie your boat down, ropes work well enough, but cam straps are quicker and more reliable. Whatever you use, securely tying a boat onto your roof racks is pretty easy. As long as you don't strap it down at its widest point, your kayak will

resist flying off. If you're tying down a plastic boat, don't be afraid to give the straps a good yank to tighten it up. On the other hand, composite boats require a more a delicate touch. In fact, I would highly recommend investing in some kayak cradles for your rack if you have a composite boat. Once you have the main straps tied securely, an extra piece of insurance involves tying lines from your bow and stern to the ends of your vehicle to prevent the kayak(s) from shooting forward and backward.

Kayak cradles being used here help hold your boat in place and prevent the hull of your kayak from deforming.

If you're using ropes, the trucker's hitch is a good knot for tying a kayak securely to the racks. To use a trucker's hitch, you'll start by securing one end of your rope to the roof rack, as close to the kayak as possible, using a bowline or any other stable knot. You'll then pass the rope over the kayak and then somewhere near the top make a simple loop by pinching a small section of the rope (called taking a bight) and then twisting it twice. Holding the loop securely, take the free end of the rope, pass it under the roof rack and bring it back up and through the loop you created. Now when you pull down on the free end of the rope, you'll tighten the hold on the kayak. You can then tie the working end of your rope off with a few half hitches.

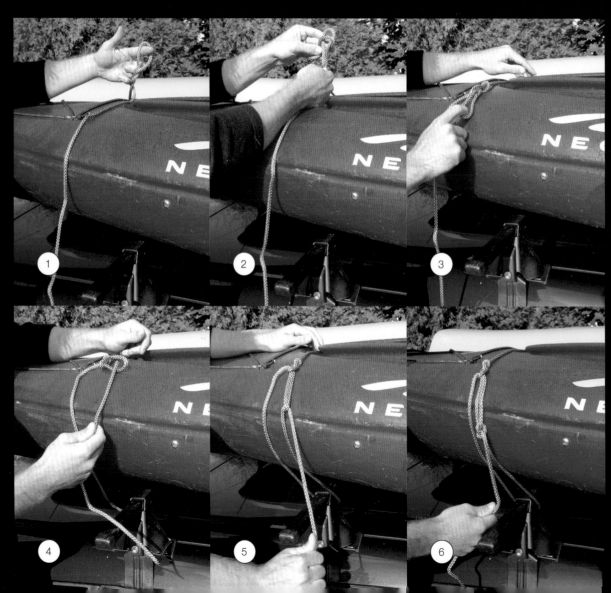

LIFTING AND CARRYING YOUR KAYAK

Although I firmly believe that kayaks are one of the most practical and user-friendly watercraft out there, it's easy to question this theory when it comes time to lift and carry your kayak. Even though kayaks are not particularly heavy, carrying anything ten to twenty feet in length is going to be challenging—and maybe dangerous to those around you!

The great thing about plastic kayaks is, that if you need to, you can get away with dragging your boat to the water; dragging any other type of boat isn't a good option. Of course, dragging your plastic kayak will give it a used look very quickly, but sometimes it's just the easiest way to get where you want to go.

The best way to carry a boat is with the help of a friend—one of you at each end. The handles at the ends of kayaks make it easy to carry two kayaks at the same time this way.

The two-person carry is the easiest means of moving kayaks around.

1. Lift the kayak onto your thighs with the cockpit out.

2. Grab the far edge, thumb out, with the hand that's on the same side as the shoulder where the boat will sit.

3. Use your knee to kick the boat up and roll it up onto your shoulder.

4. Don't forget to make wide turns when carrying a boat solo.

A kayak cart provides the easiest means of moving a boat around: it's designed to break down easily for storing in the kayak while you're paddling.

An option for stronger people using a sit-inside kayak is to carry the boat solo with the cockpit coaming sitting on your shoulder. The challenge is usually in getting the kayak onto your shoulder in the first place. To get the kayak on your shoulder, bend your legs and keep your back as straight as possible. Lift the boat onto your thighs, cockpit facing away from you. Next, grab the far edge of the cockpit coaming. In one smooth movement, kick the boat up with your knee and roll it onto your shoulder. To put the kayak back down, simply reverse these steps. If you don't have far to go and your boat isn't too heavy, you can also carry a boat like a suitcase from the center of the cockpit.

A final great option for moving a kayak around is a kayak cart. Kayak carts are basically cradles with two wheels that support the kayak so that you can simply grab an end and tow your boat behind you. Carts are great because they're easy to assemble and then can be packed down and stored inside your boat while you're on the water.

WARMING UP AND STRETCHING

Although kayaking is a very low-impact sport and you really don't need to be in great shape to enjoy it, you do need to be kind to your body. After all, it's the engine that powers your paddle and drives your boat, so you need to keep it running smoothly.

As with any physical activity, it's important to take the time to allow your body to warm up, so resist the urge to sprint away from the beach at full throttle. Of course, the type of warm-up and stretching you should do is directly related to the type of paddling you'll be doing. If you're just heading out on the water to do some fishing or for a casual paddle to enjoy some afternoon sun, you're not going to need a real warm-up or stretching (although stretching is never a bad idea). If you're going to be paddling more aggressively though, you'll want to incorporate a warm-up and stretching routine into your day.

The idea behind warming up is to slowly warm your core body temperature, which has the effect of improving your coordination and body elasticity, and stimulating your respiratory and cardiovascular systems. A good general warm-up should involve joint rotations, starting with your feet and working your way up. This means performing slow circular movements, both clockwise and counter-clockwise, until those joints seem to move smoothly. Next, you'll do a few minutes of light aerobic activity to start slightly elevating your heart rate. A short, light jog works well.

Once you're warmed up, you can begin some light stretching. It is not a good idea to stretch before your muscles are warm! Don't forget to stretch your lower body as well as your upper body. Tight hamstrings are one of the most common reasons that paddlers experience discomfort when kayaking. When stretching, work each stretch from at least twenty seconds to a full minute, while breathing slowly and deeply. Make sure you don't force positions that hurt in any way. Stretching shouldn't be a painful experience.

Stretching before a workout loosens stiff muscles and gets the muscles ready to work; it isn't the time to try to increase your flexibility. The time to stretch to increase your flexibility is at the end of a workout, during your body's cool-down period.

Did You Know?

PADDLING SAFETY AND COMMON SENSE

As I've already mentioned, kayaking is a remarkably safe and user-friendly activity. In fact, compared to most other outdoor activities, the chances of getting hurt while kayaking are very small. With that said, it is important to understand that when things do go wrong during kayaking, the fact that you're on the water means that situations can become very serious, very fast. It's for this reason that it is important that you understand and appreciate the risks and hazards involved with kayaking, and that you assume a conservative and safety-conscious attitude when making decisions on the water.

Avoiding dangerous situations on the water is surprisingly easy. First and foremost, understand that alcohol and boating simply don't go together. Regrettably, alcohol is a major factor in boating accidents. It's also critical that you wear a PFD whenever you're on the water. By investing in a kayaking-specific PFD designed to be as comfortable and unrestricting as possible while you're seated and paddling in a kayak, you'll eliminate most reasons for wanting to remove it. On a similar note, you need to dress for the conditions. Cold water represents the biggest hazard, because immersion in cold water can quickly result in hypothermia. If you're paddling in cold water, you need to be more conservative in all your decisions. Paddle only in calm conditions, stay close to shore, never paddle alone, and keep in mind that you're better off overdressing and being too warm than being too cold. With all that cold water around, it's easy to cool yourself off!

CHOOSING A GOOD PADDLING LOCATION

One of the easiest ways to stay safe and ensure that your paddling experience is fun for everyone is to choose an appropriate paddling location. One of the greatest things about kayaking is that there are so many great spots to explore, whether you live near a lake, river, pond or the ocean. Most importantly, you'll want to pick a location that's sheltered from both wind and waves. Although the ocean and large lakes can sometimes be incredibly calm and provide an ideal kayaking environment, it's important to recognize that conditions can quickly change. If you choose to paddle in exposed areas, where conditions can deteriorate really quickly, you should always check the weather forecast before heading out, and keep your eyes open for signs of bad weather moving in while you're paddling, whether it's forecasted or not. Also, make sure that you know of a variety of different takeout points so that you won't feel compelled to challenge the elements just to get back to the one place you know you can get out.

The ideal kayaking environment has a good access point for launching, lots of places to easily go ashore and minimal motorized on-water traffic. Look for calm bays or quiet lakes and riverways. Although it can be tempting to search out the most remote location possible, bear in mind that if you ever did need a little assistance, it's awfully nice to know there will be someone around who can lend a hand.

PADDLING ALONE

Although there are some people who thrive on the feeling of doing outdoor activities alone, as a general rule, paddling alone is a bad idea for the simple reason that when things do go wrong on the water, situations can become life threatening. Having a friend close by to help out could make a huge difference some day. If you insist on paddling alone, it would be prudent to take a sea kayaking safety and rescue course and learn self-rescue techniques, like rolling a kayak. Of course, you can't let this new-found knowledge encourage you to push your limits too much, whether you're paddling alone or not. I see this a lot with developing whitewater kayakers. Oftentimes, when whitewater kayakers first learn their roll, they start pushing their limits too far and put themselves into more dangerous situations than before they learned to roll.

The bottom line is, if you do decide to paddle alone, you need to be even more conservative than normal with all the decisions you make: you need to stay more alert and aware of your surroundings to minimize the chances of getting caught off guard and being left in a compromising position.

CHAPTER THREE

THE ESSENTIALS

LAUNCHING AND LANDING

USING YOUR PADDLE

WET EXIT

THREE GOLDEN RULES

BALANCE ON EDGE

LAUNCHING AND LANDING

In most cases, launching or landing your kayak is fairly straightforward. The trick is to move as quickly as possible into a sitting position.

Beaches are the easiest spots to get into and out of your kayak. On a nice sandy beach, you can hop into your boat with it resting at the edge of the water and then just push yourself out with your hands when you're ready. If you're in a composite boat and concerned about scratches, you can also get into your boat while it floats in a few inches of water by straddling it and then just dropping your butt into the seat. If you're on a beach with a little bit of shore break washing in, make sure to keep your boat pointed directly into the waves when you get in. If you let your kayak turn sideways at all, the waves will swipe your boat sideways—and out of your control.

1. When getting in from a dock, start from a sitting position with your feet in the boat.
2. Turn towards the bow and place both hands firmly on the dock.
3. Sit down as quickly as possible into the seat.
4. Once settled, grab your paddle and push away from the dock.

For rocky launch sites, use your paddle as an outrigger for support as you slide into or onto your boat.

If your launch site requires that you get into your boat from a dock, choose the dock's lowest point for the task. The higher the dock, the more difficult getting in will be. Start by positioning your kayak parallel to the dock and then sit down on the dock beside the kayak's seat. Make sure you place your paddle close by, so it will be within easy reach once you're in your boat. With your feet centered in the kayak, turn your body towards the bow, place both hands on the dock, and then quickly lower yourself into the seat. To get out, you'll reverse these steps.

For awkward or rocky launch sites, the best way to get into your boat involves floating your kayak in the water and using your paddle as an outrigger for support. This means placing your paddle at ninety degrees to the kayak with the shaft resting on the boat just behind the cockpit and the far blade supported on shore. You'll then grab the paddle shaft and coaming behind your back and squat down beside the kayak. Cheating your weight onto the outrigger, slip your legs into the boat and drop your butt into the seat. You can get out of your kayak on uneven or rocky shorelines using this same technique in reverse, although it will be difficult if you have any waves to contend with.

SEAL LAUNCH

Pete Darrah does the seldom-seen beaver dam seal launch.

Seal launching off the high sides of this fishing boat ended up being the easiest way to get on the water.

Sometimes, the easiest way to get into the water is to get in your boat on land and then slide right in—which is called seal launching. The seal launch is a fun way to start your day, although it does carry some risk and it's definitely not a technique to use in anything other than a plastic kayak. You can seal launch off almost anything, from a grassy hill to a rocky beach, and even off the side of a boat. Expert whitewater kayakers will sometimes even seal launch off cliffs as a means of entering a canyon that is otherwise inaccessible. Of course, a botched seal launch from any significant height is a great way to hurt yourself or break your gear.

Seal launching is a skill like any other, and just as a whitewater kayaker wouldn't start by running a waterfall, you shouldn't start with a large seal launch. Regardless of how big the seal launch is, you have to be prepared for flipping, because there's a good chance that that's exactly what will happen unless you have a reliable brace in your arsenal.

USING YOUR PADDLE

Over time, your paddle will evolve into an extension of your arms and it's probably fair to say that it is the piece of gear you will become most intimate with. We've already talked about the different types of paddles, as well as how to choose the right one for your type of kayak, so now let's look at how to use it.

A kayak paddle should be held with your hands an equal distance from the blades and slightly more than shoulder-width apart. Having your hands too far out makes for awkward strokes, while having your hands too far in toward the center will cost you substantially in the amount of force you can apply at the blades. A

great way to establish the correct hand placement is to position the center of the paddle on top of your head and then grip the paddle so your elbows are bent at approximately ninety degrees.

Knowing roughly where your hands should be, the next thing to look at is whether or not your paddle has any feather to contend with. Feathered paddles have blades offset at different angles. As one blade pulls through the water, the angle of the other blade allows it to slice through any wind. Feathered paddles are traditional and can make a small difference if you're paddling in an area with high winds, but they are less intuitive to use and by no means essential. We're going to now look at how to use a heavily feathered paddle since the same concept gets applied when using an unfeathered paddle, but to a lesser extent.

First of all, being left- or right-handed has an important impact on your paddling, as it dictates your control hand. For a right-handed paddler, the control hand is the right; for a left-handed paddler, the control hand is the left. Having said this, it's becoming increasingly more common for all paddlers to learn with right-handed control paddles. The

With your hands an equal distance from the blades and your paddle on top of your head, your arms should be bent at ninety degrees.

If the right hand is the control hand, it should retain a firm grip with the big knuckles aligned with the top edge of the paddle blade.

The left hand stays loose so that after a stroke on the right is taken, the shaft can rotate in the left hand so the left blade can be planted squarely in the water.

reason is simple: left-handed control paddles are very uncommon, so finding a replacement is highly unlikely in the event that you break, forget, or lose your paddle. Your control hand is the hand that grips the shaft firmly at all times, which is why we also call it the "glue" hand. The opposite hand, in contrast, is often referred to as the "grease" hand. The control hand's grip should never change whether you're forward paddling, back paddling, or even rolling your kayak. It's your reference point for how the paddle will react and you need to be able to rely on it automatically. The big knuckles of your control hand should be

aligned with the top edge of your paddle blade. After taking a stroke with your control hand side, you'll loosen your grip with your grease hand so that you can rotate the shaft within it. The rotation is necessary to accommodate the feather of your paddle and lets you place the next blade in the water squarely. This loosening of the grease hand and the rotation of the shaft within it takes place between each stroke.

If you're using a paddle with no feather you can get away with not rotating the paddle between each stroke. However, it's ideal to use this same technique in a

scaled-back way because there's naturally a small amount of rotation associated with paddling. If you don't let the paddle shaft rotate a little in your grease (non-control) hand, you'll find that wrist doing small curls while you paddle, which can take a toll on your body over time.

On a final note, it's important that you keep your control hand grip on the paddle secure, but as light as possible. A light grip will let you paddle more comfortably for longer periods of time, and is instrumental for avoiding overuse injuries such as tendonitis in the wrist and elbow.

WET EXIT

A wet exit refers to the act of getting out of your kayak when it's upside down, and it's one of the first skills that anyone using a sea or whitewater kayak should learn. The reason it's important is not because it's difficult to do, but because these boats have smaller cockpits with aggressive thigh hooks, and you'll feel much more comfortable and confident paddling if you've taken the time to practice the wet exit—especially if you're using a skirt. If you're paddling a recreational kayak, there isn't the same compelling reason to practice the wet exit because if you flip, you're not going to have a choice. You're going to fall out of the boat whether you want to or not, because the cockpit is big and there's almost nothing to hold you in.

Here's how the wet exit works, assuming you're wearing a skirt. The entire process of wet exiting will only take a few seconds, and the more relaxed you are, the more smoothly it'll all go. The first thing you'll do after flipping upside down is lean forward and find your skirt's rip cord with one hand, while the other hand hangs firmly on to your paddle. Now yank the rip cord forward and up to pop your skirt. Next, slide your hands back to your hips (still holding the paddle), and while staying leaning forward, push yourself out. You'll end up doing a bit of a forward somersault out of the boat.

The trickiest part of this maneuver is fighting the instinct to lean back as you slide out of your kayak. The problem with leaning back is that it raises your butt off the seat and presses your thighs against the thigh hooks, which will actually make it harder to slide out, and slows down your wet exit.

The wet exit only needs to be considered by those paddling sea kayaks or whitewater kayaks, which have small cockpits.

THREE GOLDEN RULES

The three "golden rules" are a set of principles that, when followed, will help you paddle the most efficiently, comfortably and safely, whether you're doing a quick paddle around the lake, riding the ocean surf, or challenging a river's whitewater.

You need to:

Use a cooperative division of the body.
Maintain the power position.
Rotate your torso.

#1 USE COOPERATIVE DIVISION OF THE BODY

Cooperative division of the body means that while the upper half of your body performs one task, the lower body can perform a totally separate one. This separation comes from the hips which should stay loose and relaxed. With loose hips, you can keep your head centered and body balanced over the kayak. This separation also lets the kayak "go with the flow" while your upper body maintains a balanced position on top.

As the lower body tilts the boat on edge, the upper body plants an aggressive bow draw.

#2 MAINTAIN THE POWER POSITION

Maintaining a power position simply means keeping your hands in front of your body, which will make your strokes the most powerful and efficient. It also offers the benefit of keeping your shoulders safe from serious injury, like a dislocation, particularly if you're getting into more dynamic types of kayaking.

Another way to think of maintaining your power position is that your arms, chest and paddle form a box when you hold your paddle in front of you. You'll maintain this box when taking any type of stroke. That doesn't mean you can't reach to the back of your boat to take a stroke. It just means that in order to do so, you'll need to rotate your whole upper body so that your hands stay in front of you. This act of rotating the upper body is fittingly named torso rotation, and it's a key concept to learn—so much so that it's our third golden rule!

By rotating the upper body while taking a reverse sweep stroke, the power position is maintained and more power is harnessed for the stroke.

#3 ROTATE YOUR TORSO

Your paddle strokes should use much more than just your arm and shoulder muscles. By using the power of your whole upper body, you'll be able to paddle much more efficiently, and it's through torso rotation that you do so. Torso rotation involves twisting at the waist as you take strokes, rather than just pulling with your arms. How to use torso rotation in specific strokes is discussed in Chapter 4, Strokes.

BALANCE ON EDGE

Edging your kayak is a great skill to learn, as it builds your comfort level and helps you manage any waves you might encounter. Edging also lets you turn most recreational and sea kayaks more easily than if they are sitting flat on the water because it lifts your keel. The keel is the downward-pointing edge on the hull of the boat, which is most evident at the ends. The keel is there to help the kayak track (travel in a straight line).

The key to edging your kayak is to apply the first golden rule—stay loose at the hips and let your upper and lower body work independently, but cooperatively. Keeping your body upright, shift your weight slightly over onto one butt cheek. You should feel your whole rib cage shifting over to the side of your kayak and your stomach and side muscles will be working a little bit to keep your body upright as you do so. If your kayak has thigh hooks, you've got a distinct advantage here because you can help stabilize the boat on edge by lifting with the opposite knee.

Staying loose at the hips is the key to edging a kayak because it lets you keep your head and weight over the kayak, even when it's held aggressively on edge.

CHAPTER FOUR

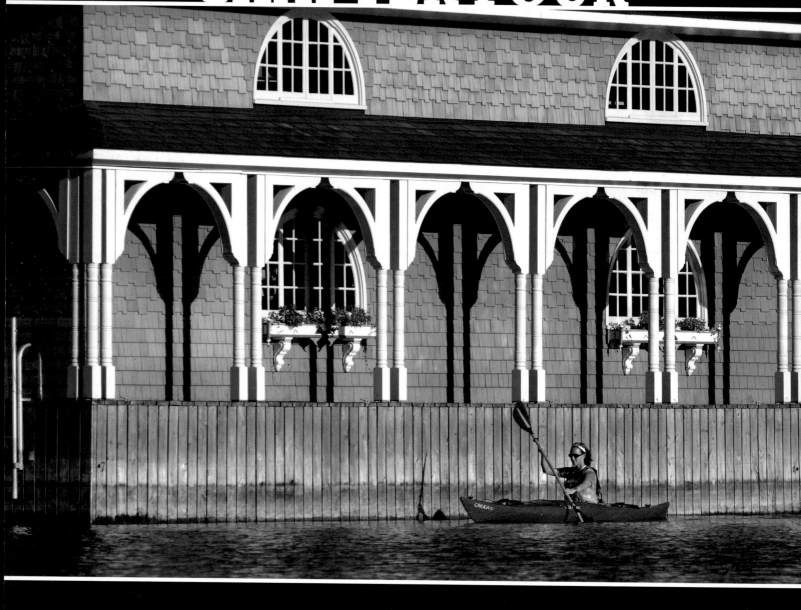

STROKES

PROPULSION STROKES

TURNING STROKES

LATERAL STROKES

STABILITY / BRACING STROKES

While kayaking is generally very intuitive, there are some key strokes worth taking the time to learn properly because they'll allow you to travel on the water most efficiently and maneuver more effectively. They'll also provide a dramatic boost to your confidence, which will let you relax and enjoy your time on the water, and which can open the doors to kayaking in more dynamic or exotic environments.

In this chapter, we're going to look at the proper technique for performing all the main strokes. In the following Maneuvers chapter, we'll look at how these strokes are applied to get either single or tandem kayaks to perform a desired action.

PROPULSION STROKES

FORWARD STROKE

The *forward stroke* is the most important stroke, for obvious reasons. Although any stroke that gets your kayak moving forward is fine, by learning correct technique you'll be able to get where you want to go with the least amount of wasted effort. Proper technique can also help prevent overuse or stress related injuries.

We're going to break down the forward stroke in three parts: the catch, rotation, and recovery.

1. Rotate your upper body and reach to plant your blade at your toes.

2. Make sure your blade is fully planted in the water before pulling on it.

3. Notice how much the upper body rotates during the forward stroke.

4. Your blade slices out of the water as it reaches your hip and you'll rotate your upper body to plant the next stroke.

The Catch

The catch is the all-important start to the forward stroke, where your paddle blade is planted in the water. Sitting up straight, with a relaxed grip on your paddle, reach to your toes and plant your blade fully into the water. This reaching action involves both your arms and your shoulders. You don't want to lean forward at the waist to reach to your toes, but rather twist from the waist. If you're reaching for a stroke with your right blade, push your right shoulder forward while reaching with your right arm. This shoulder-reach causes you to rotate or wind up your upper torso and is commonly referred to as torso rotation (our 3rd Golden Rule.) As I already mentioned, torso rotation lets you harness the power of your front and side stomach muscles for your strokes, rather than just using your arms. With your body wound up, spear your blade into the water so the whole blade is submerged. Once that blade is completely in the water, pull on your paddle and unwind your upper body to drive your boat forward.

One of the most common mistakes is pulling on the forward stroke before the blade is fully planted in the water. If you do this, your strokes will create a lot of splash, which means that you're actually wasting energy pulling water past your kayak, rather than pulling your kayak forward through the water. To understand it better, imagine that you're planting your paddle in cement when you take a stroke. The paddle shouldn't really move anywhere once it's planted. Think of pulling yourself past that paddle. The only way this will work is if you have fully and securely planted your whole blade in the water.

The catch involves rotating your upper body and reaching to plant the blade fully in the water before you pull on it.

Notice how much the upper body has rotated during the forward stroke.

Rotation

Your body is like an elastic band in that once it's wound up, you'll have a lot of potential energy at your command. Rotation refers to the way you'll use the energy to power your forward stroke.

As described above, when taking a forward stroke, your body gets wound up and your paddle is planted at your toes. You'll now pull on your paddle and drive your kayak forward using as much of your large torso muscles as possible, rather than relying on your comparatively weak arms to do the work. In fact, a good way to think about it is that your arms are just a supplement to the power of your torso. True power comes from your stomach, side, and back muscles.

Did You Know?

For maximum forward stroke drive, try pushing with the foot on the same side that you're taking a forward stroke on. This helps you transfer more power to your stroke.

Now that you're engaging the most powerful muscles, let's take a quick look at what the rest of your body will be doing. With elbows bent and staying low, pull on the paddle with your arms as you take each stroke. The range of motion that your arms use should actually be quite small, since your torso will be doing the bulk of the work. As a general rule, the more vertical the paddle shaft is while taking a forward stroke, the more power you'll get from it. To make the paddle more vertical, bring your top hand higher and further across your boat. Keep in mind that these sprinting strokes are great when you're in a hurry, but they're also very tiring. For general paddling, keep your top hand about shoulder or chest level.

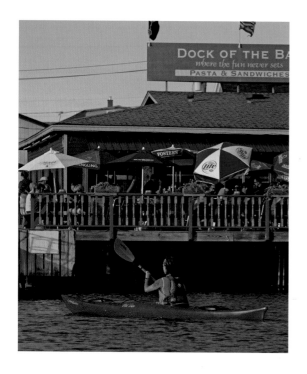

Did You Know?

To develop a better understanding of how important torso rotation is for powering your forward stroke, try paddling forward with your arms locked completely straight at the elbows. Although it won't be comfortable to paddle like this, you can really get your boat moving using only the rotation of your torso to power your kayak forward.

Recovery

The recovery is the point at which your forward stroke ends and the blade gets removed from the water. This happens when your bottom hand reaches your hip, which is earlier than most paddlers expect or practice. When your stroke reaches your hip, slice your paddle up out of the water sideways and get ready for the next stroke. At this point, your body should have unwound past its position of rest and be wound up ready for the next catch of your other blade on the opposite side. Plant your blade deeply into the water and then pull the next stroke through.

Now that you have all the pieces for an efficient and powerful forward stroke, try to put them all together as smoothly as possible while keeping your boat as "quiet" as you can. A quiet boat has minimal bob from side to side or up and down and will glide through the water most efficiently.

The stroke ends and your blade should be fully out of the water by the time your bottom hand is in line with your hip.

REVERSE STROKE

Although you might not use the reverse stroke very often, it can come in handy when maneuvering in confined spaces and is definitely worth learning. Also, from a fitness perspective reverse strokes are great to practice because they work different muscles, which provides a more balanced body workout.

The reverse stroke is just like the forward stroke, only done in reverse. However, that doesn't mean that you spin the paddle in your hands when performing the stroke. Instead, your grip on the shaft remains the same as always, and you use the back face of the paddle blade to push water.

The reverse stroke starts just behind your hip and ends at your toes. To start, hold your top hand in a relaxed position in front of your body between chest and chin height. As you plant your blade deeply in the water behind your hip, turn your upper body in that same direction. With your body rotated towards your paddle, you can use the power of torso rotation to help your stroke by unwinding your body as you push your blade towards the bow. As your stroke reaches your toes, your body should be wound up in the other direction and ready for the next stroke on the opposite side.

1. Rotating your upper body aggressively, plant the reverse stroke fully in the water just behind your hip.

2. Notice the arms stay in a relatively fixed position, because torso rotation provides the bulk of the power for the stroke.

3. The reverse stroke ends when your blade reaches your toes.

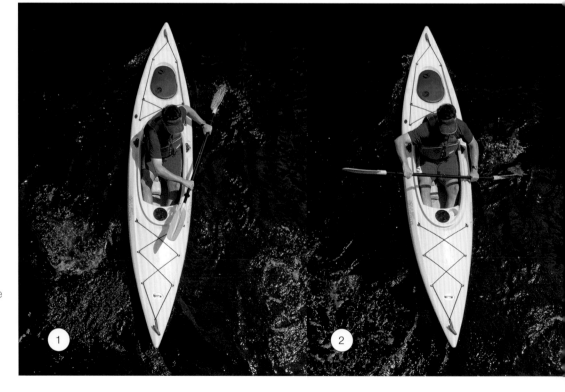

As a final note, when reversing, always be sure and keep an eye on where you're going, or you're sure to collide with something or someone. I like to look over my shoulder every few strokes and it's easiest to do this by turning my head to the same side as my stroke, taking a quick glance over that shoulder just as I plant my blade in the water.

STOPPING—THE REVERSE STROKE AS A BRAKE

The best way to put on the brakes and stop is with braking strokes, which are short and quick alternating reverse strokes. You should be able to come to a complete stop with just three of these strokes. This is another good skill to practice so that you're prepared to use it if you ever really need it.

The author puts on the brakes with a powerful reverse stroke.

TURNING STROKES

Most recreational, touring and sea kayaks are designed to travel well in a straight line, which means that you can't expect them to turn on a dime. When you do need to turn them, you'll use one of four strokes: forward sweep, reverse sweep, bow draw, or stern rudder.

FORWARD SWEEP

The forward sweep stroke is the best way to turn your kayak when sitting still. It's also an excellent way to make course corrections when you're in motion, because it allows you to turn your boat while keeping your speed going, rather than killing all your forward momentum.

Just like the forward stroke, the forward sweep starts with your body wound up and your blade completely in the water at your toes. It also harnesses the power of torso rotation. Unlike the forward propelling stroke, your hands will stay very low during the sweep and your blade will follow an arcing path as far out to the side of your kayak as possible. To do this, the hand controlling the active blade will reach out over the water, while the other maintains a low position in front of your stomach. Your blade will continue on its arcing path until it approaches the stern of your boat. You'll then slice your paddle out of the water before it touches the stern and move to your next stroke.

To get the most power from your torso rotation, sit upright in your kayak and watch your active blade throughout its arc. Following the blade with your eyes will force your upper body to rotate throughout the stroke. You can also push off the foot pedal on the sweeping-stroke side of the boat for even more power.

1. The forward sweep starts with your body wound up and your paddle planted deeply at your toes with the shaft held low.

2. Keeping your hands low, sweep an arcing path far out to the side of the kayak.

3. Follow your active blade with your eyes to help incorporate torso rotation into the stroke.

4. Finish your sweep before your paddle hits the stern of your kayak.

REVERSE SWEEP

The reverse sweep is exactly what it sounds like—a forward sweep stroke done in reverse, and like the back stroke, you'll use the back face of your paddle. Like the forward sweep, the reverse sweep can be used while stationary or when traveling forward, but it's important to note that it will kill almost all of your speed. This aspect of it can be helpful when you need to put on the brakes and make a major course correction.

The reverse sweep begins with your body wound up and your blade completely in the water at the stern of your kayak, about six inches away from the hull. In order to get the most torso rotation possible into your stroke, keep your eyes on your active paddle blade. With your blade planted deeply in the water, sweep a wide arc all the way out to the side of your kayak and up to your toes. The hand controlling the active blade reaches out over the water, while the other takes a position in front of your stomach. Track the progress of your blade by watching it throughout its arc. By keeping your head turning with your active blade, you will encourage good torso rotation and ensure that your body unwinds throughout the whole stroke.

Once you're comfortable with both the forward and reverse sweeps, try combining a forward sweep on one side with a reverse sweep on the opposite side. You'll find that this combination of strokes is so effective that you can just about spin your kayak on the spot.

1. The reverse sweep starts at the stern of your kayak with your head and body aggressively rotated towards it.

2. Keeping your hands low, sweep a wide arc with your paddle.

3. Notice the arms have stayed in a relatively fixed position throughout the stroke, which means torso rotation is providing much of the power.

4. The stroke ends after having swept a full, wide arc.

Sweeping on Edge

As mentioned in the section on Balance on Edge, putting your kayak on edge lets it turn more easily. So, once you're comfortable sweeping with your boat kept flat, it's time to add some boat tilt to the equation to make your sweep stroke its most effective. Whether you're using a forward or reverse sweep stroke, you'll tilt your kayak on edge towards your active sweeping blade.

STERN RUDDER

Stern rudders are the most powerful way to control your kayak when moving forward. There are two forms of the stern rudder: the stern pry, and the stern draw. Both strokes start from the same position—with your paddle planted firmly in the water behind your body and parallel to your kayak. To do this, and still keep your hands in front of your body in the power position (Golden Rule #2), you'll need to use some aggressive torso rotation (Golden Rule #3), which means turning your whole upper body towards your rudder. Your front hand should be held comfortably in front of your chest. From this position you can either push away with the backside of your paddle blade, which is called a stern pry, or you can draw water towards your stern with its power face, which is called the stern draw. The stern pry is by far the more powerful of the two strokes and the most commonly used.

The stern pry involves pushing away with the backside of your paddle; it's the most powerful way to control your kayak when moving forward.

BOW DRAW

The bow draw is used to turn the bow of your kayak. It's not a very practical turning stroke when your kayak is sitting still, but it can be a very useful stroke for making moving/carving turns (as will be discussed in the next chapter.) As a general rule, the shorter your kayak is, the more effective your bow draw will be.

The bow draw gets planted about a foot and a half out to the side of your toes, with your wrists cocked back so that the power face of your active blade faces the bow of your kayak. You'll then pull the blade in towards your toes where the stroke ends.

A bow draw turn in action.

LATERAL STROKES

Lateral strokes are used to move your kayak sideways and are amazingly useful maneuvering strokes for pulling yourself up beside a dock, or whenever you want to close the distance between yourself and another paddler.

BASIC DRAW

The basic draw involves reaching out to the side of your hip, planting your blade, and then pulling your boat and body sideways toward it. For the most effective stroke, plant your blade completely in the water, rotate your head and upper body to face your active blade, and get your paddle shaft as vertical as possible. Getting your paddle shaft vertical will require reaching across your upper body with your top hand, which takes good balance, so you might want to start by practicing your draw stroke with your top hand in front of your face. When your blade is completely in the water, pull your lower hand in towards your hip. Your top hand will stay very stationary, acting as the pivot point for the stroke. Before your paddle hits your boat, you'll need to finish the stroke by slicing the blade out of the water towards the stern. The paddle should exit about six inches away from the side. Be careful that you

1. Draw strokes are used to move your kayak sideways.

2. With your head and upper body turned to face the active blade, plant the draw stroke about two feet straight out from your hip.

3. The draw stroke ends before your paddle hits your boat.

4. Slice the paddle out of the water towards the stern of the kayak and you're ready for your next stroke.

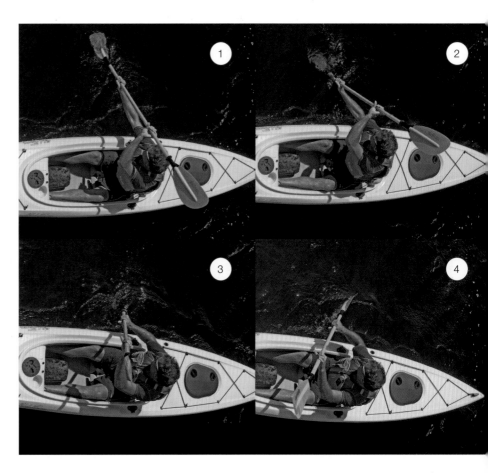

do not bring your paddle too close to the side of your kayak before finishing the stroke. If you do pin the paddle up against your kayak, it can easily lever your boat upside down, flipping you with surprising speed!

One of the most common problems people have with the draw stroke is finding that it turns their kayak, rather than moving it only sideways. If you experience this problem, it generally means that you're using your draw stroke too far forward or too far back. If you're pulling your draw too far forward (towards your knee instead of your hip) you'll pull your bow towards your paddle. If your draw is too far back, you'll pull your stern towards your paddle. Drawing your paddle towards your hip is a good guideline, but every kayak reacts differently and you can expect to need to make some fine adjustments to keep your boat moving perfectly sideways.

Did You Know?

Once you're comfortable with this basic draw stroke, you're ready for the T-stroke. The only difference between the two is that instead of slicing the blade out of the water towards the stern, you'll keep your active blade in the water as you move it back to its starting point. To do this, after pulling in towards your hip, you'll curl your wrists forward to turn your blade ninety degrees so that you can effortlessly slice it back out to the side of your kayak.

SCULLING DRAW

The sculling draw is set up in the same way as the basic draw—with your upper body rotated towards it, your paddle shaft positioned as vertically as possible, and your blade fully planted in the water at ninety degrees from your hip. The difference between the two strokes lies in how you'll pull on your paddle. Instead of pulling your blade directly into your hip, you'll use something called a sculling motion. This sculling motion lets you pull steadily on your paddle and bypasses the recovery phase that the basic draw stroke requires.

The key to sculling is keeping your paddle blade moving along a short path forward and backward about a foot or two out to the side of your kayak, with a blade angle that opens your power face to the oncoming water and pulls your paddle away from your kayak. This unique blade angle is commonly referred to as a "climbing angle". Climbing angle means that the leading edge of your paddle blade is higher than the trailing edge. It's the same as spreading jam on toast: picture the knife's angle as it glides over

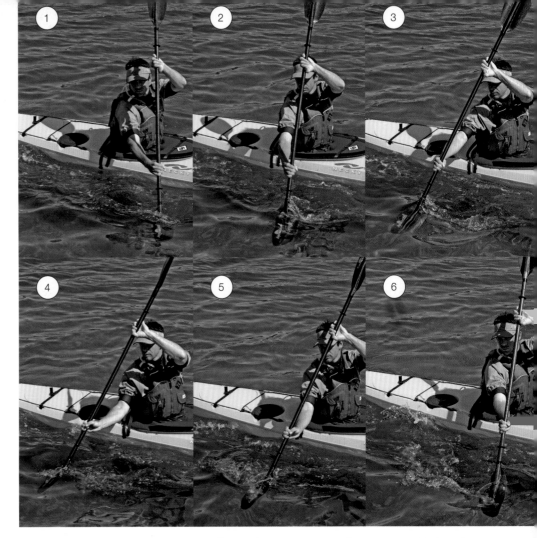

The sculling draw is a much more powerful draw than the basic draw, but it requires significantly more paddle dexterity—which is why it's a great stroke to learn!

the bread's surface, leading edge higher than the trailing edge. To maintain a climbing angle on your blade while performing the sculling draw you'll cock your wrists slightly back as you slice your blade forward. You'll then make a quick transition and curl your wrists slightly forward as you slice your blade backward. Keep in mind that the change in blade angle is subtle. If you open your power face too much, you'll be pushing your kayak forward and backward rather than drawing it sideways.

Using this sculling technique, you can apply steady drawing pressure with your paddle blade and move your boat laterally at a surprising speed. Don't forget that, just like any other stroke, the power for your sculling draw comes from your torso rotation. This is why it's so important that you turn your body aggressively into the stroke. The forward and backward movement of your paddle can then be driven by your torso rotation, while your arms stay in a relatively fixed position.

STABILITY / BRACING STROKES

Bracing is used to recover when you've been thrown off balance, and although you can use it fairly effectively while paddling a recreational kayak, it's a much more important skill to learn if you're paddling a sea, touring, or whitewater kayak, because the outfitting in these boats (thigh hooks in particular) make it possible to recover even after your boat has flipped almost completely upside down. There are two basic forms of braces: the "high" and "low" brace. Both involve reaching out to the side of your kayak with your paddle and slapping the water with one blade, which momentarily stops you from flipping and provides the support needed for your body to right the boat. The only major difference between the two is the position of your paddle.

If you're using a boat with thigh hooks, the way your body acts in order to level out your boat is counterintuitive, but absolutely essential. After slapping the water with your paddle, the natural inclination is to swing your head and body back over the top of your kayak. The problem with lifting your head up like this is that you'll inadvertently pull on your top knee, which simply flips your kayak more quickly. The only way to successfully recover using a brace is to level the kayak before swinging your head and body over top. The only way to level the kayak is by pulling up with the knee that is going underwater, and the only way to pull up with this bottom knee is to drop your head towards the water in the direction that you're flipping. To make sure that your head drops towards the water, try watching your slapping blade as you brace. It's hard to lift your head if you're looking down.

While playing in rough water, the author uses a low brace to stabilize himself.

LOW BRACE

The low brace gets its name from the fact that you'll hold it quite low. To set your paddle up for a low brace, sit upright and roll the paddle under your elbows so that your forearms are virtually vertical—in a push-up position. From here, you'll reach out to ninety degrees so that one hand is at your belly button and the other is out over the water, and then you'll then smack the water with the non-power face or backside of your paddle blade. You can't lean on a low brace because your blade will simply sink and you'll flip upsidedown, so immediately after slapping the water, slide your paddle forward and inward, and roll your knuckles upward to clear the blade from the water.

If your kayak doesn't have thigh hooks, the key to leveling off your kayak is to drop your head and body towards the water to lower your center of gravity. If you do have thigh hooks, you'll do the same thing, only you'll pull up with your lower knee at the same time to level off the kayak.

The low brace is a great reactionary brace when paddling in dynamic conditions because it can be thrown in at less than a second's notice and the low arm position keeps your shoulders really well protected from injury. For whitewater kayakers in particular, the low brace is one of the best recovery techniques.

The low brace uses the backside of your paddle against the water, which means rolling your paddle and hands into a push-up position.

Dropping your head toward the fall lets you completely right your kayak with your lower body.

Clear the blade from the water by slicing your paddle forward and upward.

1 The high brace uses the power face of your paddle against the water, which means rolling your paddle into a pull-up position.

2 Drop your head towards the water so that you can hip-snap the boat upright.

3 The high brace can be very powerful, but remember to keep your hands low and your shoulders safe.

HIGH BRACE

The high brace is similar to the low brace, only you start with your hands in a position similar to what you'd do for a pull-up. This means you'll be using the power face instead of the backside of your blades to contact the water.

Although it's called the "high" brace, you need to keep your paddle and your hands low and in front of your body to keep your shoulders safe and your bracing blade flat to the water. As you start to tip over, reach out at ninety degrees to the kayak and smack the water with the power face of the paddle. Immediately drop your head and body towards the water to lower your center of gravity and level off your kayak. If you are paddling a kayak with thigh hooks, you'll pull up with your lower knee to level the kayak at the same time.

As you perfect the high brace in a kayak with thigh hooks, you'll be amazed at how powerful it can be. Just remember that for even the biggest high braces, you've got to keep your hands low to keep your shoulders safe from injury.

CHAPTER FIVE

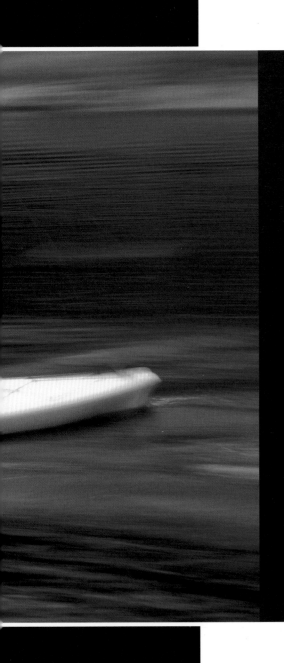

MANEUVERS

THE KAYAK IN MOTION

GOING STRAIGHT FORWARD

PIVOT TURNS

MOVING / CARVING TURNS

In this chapter we're going to look at how to make your kayak perform specific maneuvers. In some cases these maneuvers might require only a single stroke, while others may require a sequence of strokes that are linked together. We've already looked at all of the different strokes you might be called upon to use; before we dive right into the maneuvers, let's look at the characteristics of a kayak in motion. By understanding a simple theory relating to a kayak in motion, you'll have a much better understanding of why the particular stroke combinations are used.

THE KAYAK IN MOTION

I can still remember the first time that I set foot in a kayak. I was only twelve years old at the time and I was no stranger to the water. I had spent whole summers at the cottage catching turtles and frogs from the canoe. Even with that experience, I remember being captivated with how effortlessly the kayak sliced its path through the water and with how close I sat to the water. In hindsight, I'm not surprised that only two years later, my fascination blossomed into a full blown kayaking addiction.

The way a kayak carves its path through the water is magical, but there's also a practical explanation for the way a kayak in motion performs. When you understand it, the maneuvers should all make a little more sense.

As the kayak slices through the water, water is hitting its front half. The water hitting the kayak is deflected and waves (or wake) are formed. The pressure of the water hitting the front of your kayak effectively holds it in place. This

A sprint kayak is very narrow so it can slice through the water with minimal water resistance. In this picture you can clearly see the waves formed by the bow of the kayak and the absence of waves by the stern section. The lack of waves indicate that there's less water pressure holding the stern in place, so it can move more freely from side to side.

water pressure immediately disappears behind the widest point of the kayak (the center). In fact, from the center of the kayak all the way to the stern, where the kayak narrows, there is a low pressure zone, indicated by the lack of waves. The stern section of the kayak does not have nearly the same water pressure holding it in place, and so the stern can move much more freely from side to side. Now it makes sense when I say that moving turns can be initiated most effectively at the stern of your kayak.

WEATHERCOCKING

You can now better appreciate the effect of a side (beam) wind on your kayak when you're traveling forward. Since your stern can move more freely from side to side than your bow, it will get pushed around more dramatically by wind. That's why every kayak will naturally turn into the wind (called weathercocking), unless a rudder or skeg is used to hold the stern in place.

All kayaks weathercock (turn into the wind) because the stern end of the kayak is more free to move side to side and will get blown downwind more quickly than the bow.

USING RUDDERS OR SKEGS

Believe it or not, the main purpose of rudders and skegs isn't to turn a kayak, but to keep a kayak tracking (going straight) when paddling in wind. A kayak naturally wants to turn into the wind, something that's called weathercocking. The rudder or skeg counteracts that tendency. Paddling in wind without a rudder or skeg can mean that you have to take much harder strokes on one side to keep your kayak tracking.

Rudders are much more popular than skegs because they can also be used to help steer a kayak. Rudders flip down from their stored position on top of the deck, through the use of haul lines found alongside the cockpit, and are then controlled using foot pedals.

When they're needed, rudders flip down from their stored position on top of the deck and are controlled by your foot pedals.

Skegs are stored in a skeg box embedded in the stern of the kayak; they are deployed by using a slider found alongside the cockpit. Because skegs don't swivel side to side, their control comes from the depth at which they are set. The more your kayak wants to weathercock, the deeper you will set the skeg. Skegs are really only useful for tracking over long distances, so you generally don't find them on recreational kayaks, but some sea and touring kayak models come with them.

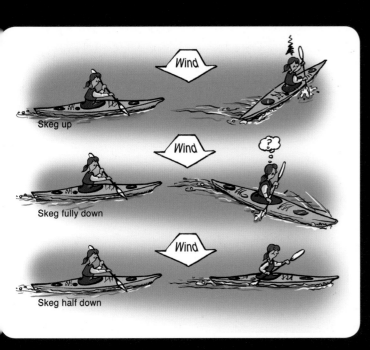

The effects of deploying a skeg at different depths.

GOING STRAIGHT FORWARD

Whitewater kayaks are designed to be as maneuverable as possible because control is more important than being able to travel effectively in a straight line when you're navigating rapids. On the flip side, recreational, touring and racing kayaks are designed to travel in a straight line as efficiently as possible. Any challenges you might have in doing so are usually the result of wind and waves, and this is where rudders or skegs can really come in handy. If you don't have a rudder or skeg, you

Tilting your kayak into the wind will help prevent it from weathercocking, although it's unreasonable to expect to hold this position for extended periods.

have a couple of options. One way to prevent your kayak from weathercocking is to paddle with your kayak tilted towards the wind. Practice this on flat water to start. Shift your weight onto a single butt cheek and hold your kayak on edge as you take regular forward strokes. What you'll find is that your kayak wants to turn slightly in the opposite direction from which you are leaning. Since weathercocking is characterized by your kayak's desire to turn into the wind, it should make sense that, to prevent your kayak from weathercocking, you should tilt your kayak slightly into the wind. Although paddling with your boat on edge is a good short term solution to weathercocking, it won't be comfortable to paddle like this over any distance. Your other option is to adjust the course you take, recognizing that paddling directly upwind or downwind is much easier than paddling with the wind hitting you from any type of angle. In many cases, the easiest way to get from A to B may not be in a straight line, but rather taking two sides of the triangle, spending as much of your time paddling directly upwind or downwind as possible.

GOING STRAIGHT IN TANDEMS

There are few tricks to paddling forward in a tandem kayak. The most efficient way of paddling a tandem is for both occupants to paddle in unison. Not only will this drive the kayak forward the quickest, you'll also avoid the clashing of paddles. If there is one paddler who is physically stronger than the other, the weaker paddler traditionally sits in the bow and dictates the paddling pace, while the stern paddler keeps pace and actively steers the kayak. In fact, if your tandem kayak has a rudder, the stern paddler will be in control of it.

PIVOT TURNS

Pivot turns mean turning your kayak when it's at a stand still. The best way to perform a pivot turn is by using a sweep stroke or a combination of sweep strokes if it's required. Either a forward sweep or reverse sweep can be used, although if you need to use multiple sweep strokes to pivot your boat, it's quickest to use alternating forward and reverse sweep strokes.

Did You Know?

To make your pivot turns even more effective, you can edge your kayak as you take your sweep strokes. Whether you're taking a forward or reverse sweep, you'll tilt your kayak towards your active sweeping blade.

TANDEM PIVOT TURNS

The trick to performing a pivot turn in a tandem kayak is for the bow paddler to take a forward sweep on one side of the kayak while the stern paddler takes a reverse sweep on the opposite of the kayak.

MOVING / CARVING TURNS

Moving or carving turns are where kayaks really shine. There are a number of ways to make carving turns and the one that you choose will usually be dictated by how aggressively you need to turn your boat. You can forward paddle on edge, use a bow draw turn, or perform a bracing lean turn.

FORWARD PADDLING ON EDGE

If you only need to make a small correction to your course, tilting your boat on edge as you continue to paddle forward might be your best course of action. What you'll find is that your kayak will carve in the opposite direction from your tilt. The more aggressively you tilt your boat, the more quickly it will turn. This technique works as effectively with tandem kayaks as it does with single kayaks.

BOW DRAW TURNS

If you need to make a slightly more aggressive carving turn, the bow draw turn might be the best solution: it is the most advanced turning technique that we'll be covering. It involves planting your paddle about a foot or two out to the side of your toes, with your wrists cocked back so that the power face catches water. You can also tilt your boat away from your draw to help get your boat turning.

This stroke can generate a lot of force, so it's important to rotate your torso to face the paddle shaft where you're performing the stroke. This protects your shoulders by keeping your arms in close to the body and in the power position. Because you're catching some water with this stroke, it will slow your boat down somewhat. As your kayak slows, draw the blade in to your toes to finish the stroke. You'll then be in a perfect position for a forward stroke to keep your forward momentum going.

The bow draw turn will probably feel a bit awkward and unbalanced at first, but as you gain confidence and balance, you will find it more and more useful. The great thing about this stroke is that it lets you make precise corrections to your course while keeping your forward paddling rhythm going—although you can't expect it to make radical course changes. If you need to turn more aggressively, you'll want to use a bracing lean turn, which we'll be looking at next.

Tandem Bow Draw Turns

To perform a bow draw turn in a tandem kayak, the bow paddler will plant the stationary bow draw while the stern paddler continues to paddle the kayak forward. It will also help to tilt the kayak away from the turn to allow the kayak to turn more efficiently.

BRACING LEAN TURNS

A bracing lean turn is a carving turn in which the kayak is held on edge while the paddle reaches out and provides both a little bracing support and turning power. Bracing lean turns are a lot more natural and powerful than bow draw turns, but they aren't designed to maintain your forward speed. They're designed to turn your kayak as effectively as possible; you'll often finish a bracing lean turn with almost no speed at all.

We're going to cover two forms of bracing lean turns; the low brace lean turn and the high brace lean turn. The only major difference between the two is the position of your brace.

Both turns start with forward sweep and are initiated with a forward sweep stroke. If you want to turn to the right, you'll use a forward sweep stroke on the left.

Low Brace Lean Turn

As soon as you've initiated the low brace lean turn with a sweep on the left, rotate your upper body to take a reverse sweep on the right, and then lean your body and tilt your boat into the stroke. The more aggressively you want to turn, the more you'll edge your kayak and push with your reverse sweep. As your boat reaches the end of its turn, your blade should have swept forward to a point directly out to the side from your hip.

A low brace lean turn.

High Brace Lean Turn

The high brace lean turn is almost the same as the low brace lean turn, only you'll be using a high brace for support, and you won't use the same reverse sweep actions. Instead, after initiating your turn with a forward sweep, plant your high brace out to the side of your kayak, just behind your hip. Of course, as we mentioned in the high brace segment, it's important that your high brace stay in a low position, with your elbow tucked in. Remember to keep a climbing angle on your active blade (by cocking your wrists back) and to level out your boat as you lose forward momentum and bracing power.

Tandem Bracing Lean Turns

Bracing lean turns in tandem kayaks are very similar to those in single kayaks. Once the stern paddler has initiated the turn, both paddlers can assume either the low brace or high brace lean turn position. Not surprisingly, the key to an effective tandem bracing lean turn is communication. The stern paddler needs to let the bow paddler know when the turn is being initiated and when the boat tilt and brace should be started.

A high brace lean turn.

CHAPTER SIX

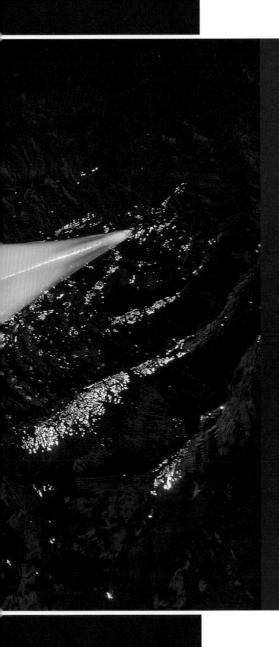

CAPSIZE RECOVERIES

BASIC RECOVERIES

SELF-RESCUES

BASIC RECOVERIES

SWIMMING

Although you might not consider swimming an actual recovery, sometimes it might be your best strategy—especially if you're paddling alone or with people who you don't think will be able to help with any other capsize recovery technique. In these cases, you should know by now that staying close to shore is the only smart thing to do.

The first thing to know about swimming is that getting your gear to shore will be a real pain in the butt unless you have a helping hand. Throw a little wind into the equation as well and you now have a royal pain in the butt, unless you're fortunate enough that the wind is blowing you and your boat directly to shore. Of course, as Murphy's Law would have it, you can almost be sure that the wind will be blowing in the other direction.

In most cases, the best strategy is to have your paddling buddy perform a boat-over-boat rescue to empty out as much of the water as possible and then flip the boat upright. Then, you can put your paddle in the empty cockpit and either swim your boat into shore, or have your friend push or tow your boat into shore for you. If you have a few people to help out, one friend can take care of your kayak and paddle, while another tows you to shore. There are a bunch of different ways to hitch a ride with a kayak. The quickest way is to simply grab the stern of the kayak and help by kicking your legs as they paddle you to shore. If the water is cold, the best way to hitch a ride is to climb onto the stern deck of the kayak and grab the paddler's waist, the bottom of their PFD, or the coaming of their cockpit. This gets the bulk of your body out of the water while you're getting towed to shore.

Did You Know?

Although you can get away with just pushing an empty boat into shore, the best way to move an empty boat is to tow it with a short tow line (sometimes called a cow tail). A tow line is attached to your body by a quick release belt that wraps around either your waist or life jacket and has a relatively short piece of webbing or rope with a carabiner on the end that can be easily clipped onto one of the grab loops of another boat. The best cow tails are made with an elastic shock cord, to make towing less jerky.

RE-ENTERING A SIT-ON-TOP KAYAK

One of the huge advantages of sit-on-top kayaks is the fact that they are so easy to get back into from the water. They make great swimming platforms—in addition to fulfilling the more standard kayak functions.

Start by positioning yourself alongside the kayak, by the seat. You can keep your paddle in one hand, slide it under your deck lines so that it doesn't get away from you, or give it to your paddling buddy. With a firm grip on the kayak, let your legs float to the surface behind you. Give a powerful kick with your legs and push with your arms to haul your chest up onto the kayak. Once you're up on the boat, twist your body around and settle into the seat. You can then swing your legs back onto the boat to complete the re-entry.

A friend can help out this re-entry process by stabilizing the kayak as you get back in. To stabilize a kayak for someone, you'll position your kayak parallel to the other, get a good grip on it, and then lean your body over onto the other kayak.

1. To get back into a sit-on-top, approach the kayak from the side and get your feet on the surface of the water behind you. Then, with a kick of the legs and a push up with the arms, draw your body on top of the kayak, keeping your weight low.

2. With the hard part accomplished, you can spin and drop your butt into the seat and then pull your legs in.

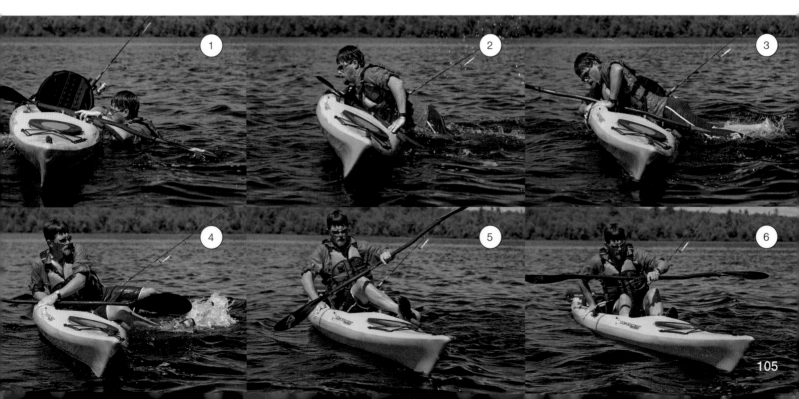

RE-ENTERING A SIT-INSIDE KAYAK

Sit-inside kayaks are more difficult to get back into from the water, but with a little practice and some help from a friend, you can learn to quickly and reliably re-enter a sit-inside too. Something to remember though is that because sit-insides aren't self-bailing, you'll have a lot of water to pump out of your kayak once you're back in the seat. This is why sea and touring kayakers carry a bilge pump, a handheld device designed to pump water from a boat. Although a bilge pump is a great piece of safety gear for any sit-inside kayak, unless you and your group are trained and practiced in on-water recoveries, you should make a habit of always paddling close enough to shore so that you can easily head to dry land and empty your boat there.

As mentioned, re-entering a sit-inside kayak from the water is more complicated. It's also more difficult, because the deck of a sit-inside kayak is higher above the water surface, which means that you'll have a harder time climbing up on it. You will be less stable once you're up there, too. Although it's possible to re-enter a sit-inside on your own, it's a technique that takes training and practice, and is beyond the scope of this book. Instead, we're going to explore a technique for re-entering a sit-inside kayak with the help of another paddler.

The first order of business is to flip your boat upright if it's upside down, in a way that minimizes the amount of water left in your kayak. This is when waterproof compartments, created by bulkheads inside your kayak, are a huge advantage.

Waterproof compartments ensure that only the cockpit area of your kayak can swamp, which makes recovering from a capsize much easier. For this reason, all sea and touring kayaks are divided into at least three waterproof compartments; a bow compartment, the cockpit area, and a stern compartment. If you're using either a sea kayak or a recreational kayak with compartments, the easiest way to flip a boat upright and minimize the amount of water inside of it is with a boat-over-boat rescue. The boat-over-boat rescue involves having the rescue boat pull up perpendicular to the bow of the capsized boat. The rescuer grabs the bow, lifts it and draws it over the deck of their kayak as the swimmer pushes downward on the stern of the capsized boat, to help lever its bow upwards. The goal here is to lift the cockpit out of the water so that it

Sea kayaks have bulkheads that divide the kayak into three waterproof compartments. Using the boat-over-boat rescue, you can empty the central cockpit compartment quite effectively before flipping the kayak upright.

can drain. As soon as you've done that, the rescuer rolls the kayak upright and off the deck of the rescue boat.

This boat-over-boat rescue will also work with kayaks that don't have bulkheads and watertight compartments, although not nearly as well. You'll still be left with a considerable amount of water in the boat. At least it can be emptied enough so the swimmer can hop back in and get to shore, where the boat can fully emptied. You could also pump the water out if you have a bilge pump, but considering the amount of effort required to pump so much water out of a kayak, you're nearly always better off heading to shore and emptying out there.

The natural thing for a swimmer to do after capsizing is to try to roll the kayak upright, but that's actually the last thing you'll want to do, especially if you're using a kayak without bulkheads and watertight compartments. When your boat has flipped upside down, air will be trapped inside, which keeps water from flooding the interior. The trapped air makes the boat-over-boat rescue much easier to perform, which is why a capsized kayak should be left upside down.

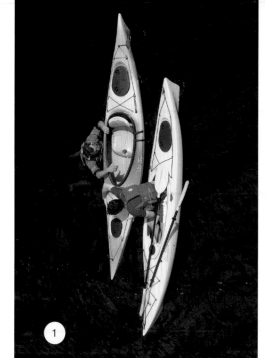

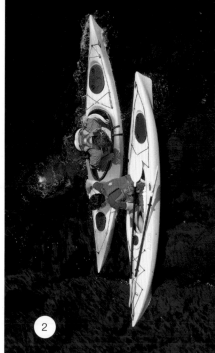

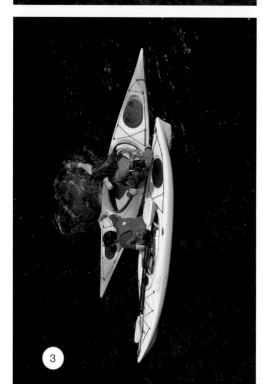

1. You'll need the help of a friend to re-enter a sit-inside kayak, unless you have amazing balance.
2. The rescuer gets a firm grip on the bow and leans their weight onto the empty boat to stabilize it while the swimmer re-enters.
3. After clambering on top of the kayak, the swimmer spins and drops their butt into the seat.
4. The rescuer needs to maintain the support of the swimmer's kayak throughout the re-entry.

With the kayak upright, your paddling partner will need to stabilize the kayak as you get back in. A partner can actually provide an incredible amount of stability, although it requires a lot of commitment. Positioning the kayak parallel to yours and getting a good grip on the empty kayak with both hands, your partner leans their whole body over onto it. As long as there's a good grip on the kayak, there's virtually no chance of flipping, because the two "rafted" kayaks will be extremely stable. You can use a very similar re-entry technique as the one outlined for the sit-on-top kayak. Position yourself alongside the kayak just behind the seat and grab the cockpit rim, which provides a good handle. Let your legs float to the surface behind you and then, with a powerful kick and push of the arms, haul your chest up and onto the kayak.

If you're re-entering a recreational kayak, which is more stable and has a significantly larger cockpit than a sea kayak, you'll be able to drop your butt into the seat and then swing your legs back into the boat. If you're re-entering a sea kayak, it's not quite so easy because the boat will be a lot less stable: unless you have very short legs, you might not be able to get your legs back in the boat if you're sitting in the seat. Draw your body onto the back deck of the kayak, just behind the cockpit. Lying chest down, turn your head towards the stern and slide your legs into the cockpit. You'll then slide into the cockpit as you twist your body to corkscrew and settle your butt back into the seat.

Because of the small cockpits on sea kayaks, you'll need to twist your body and slide your legs into the kayak before you can drop your butt into the seat.

TANDEM SIT-INSIDE RE-ENTRY

Re-entering a tandem sit-inside kayak is only more difficult than re-entering a single sit-inside kayak if the deck of the tandem is higher out of the water (which it sometimes is), because you'll need to lift your body further out of the water. It's like getting out the side of a pool with a higher edge. The bigger challenge is usually in emptying and flipping the kayak upright. The boat-over-boat rescue can be difficult when you have such a large boat swamped with water. You have to expect there to be a fair amount of water left in your boat after flipping it upright; heading to shore to fully empty the kayak will probably be your best choice. Otherwise, you'll get back into your kayak using the same re-entry technique we just looked at; it will be easiest to do so one person at a time.

Scoop Re-entry

The scoop re-entry is a technique that can be very useful if swimmers don't have the strength or mobility necessary to lift themselves back onto and into the kayak. To perform a scoop re-entry, you won't start with the boat-over-boat rescue because you actually need to keep the boat swamped. Instead, the rescuer pulls up alongside the capsized kayak, reaches over the hull and grabs the cockpit coaming. The rescuer pulls the kayak onto its side, cockpit out, and holds it there. The swimmer grabs the coaming and pulls their body into the swamped cockpit of the kayak. Once inside, the swimmer leans back to keep the center of gravity as low as possible while the rescuer pulls on the coaming to roll the kayak upright.

Of course, one of the biggest problems with the scoop re-entry is the fact that you're left with a completely swamped kayak, which is unstable and difficult to paddle. You have no choice but to hand pump the water out of the kayak with a bilge pump.

The scoop is a good rescue if the swimmer is unable to lift herself out of the water.

SELF-RESCUES

As you get more and more comfortable with paddling, there's a good chance that you'll want to explore new areas of kayaking. Part of this exploration will likely involve self-rescue skills, which will make you less dependent on others and give your overall confidence a huge boost. Two of the most common and helpful forms of self-rescue are the paddle float re-entry and the kayak roll.

PADDLE FLOAT RE-ENTRY

If you're paddling a sit-inside kayak, the paddle float re-entry is a neat self-rescue technique to have in your bag of tricks, although it should be understood from the outset that you can't rely on this rescue in anything but the calmest of conditions. In other words, just because you have a confident paddle float re-entry, don't think you can safely start traveling further from shore and into areas more exposed to wind and waves.

The paddle float re-entry uses your paddle as an outrigger for support, with a float attached to one blade to give it more buoyancy.

After swimming out of your kayak, attach your paddle float to one end of your paddle. You'll probably want to hook a foot onto your kayak to keep it close. Once the float is attached to your paddle, your next job is to flip your kayak upright while getting as little water inside as possible. The quicker you flip it upright, the better. Then, place the paddle across the back of the cockpit coaming, perpendicular to the kayak, with the paddle float in the water, as far out to the side as possible. Many sea kayaks will actually have bungee cords or lines positioned directly behind the cockpit so you can slide your blade underneath and have it stay there more easily. Now, hold the paddle and the coaming of the cockpit

in one hand and reach across to grab the coaming with the other hand, while you let your feet float to the surface behind you. With a hard kick and an aggressive push up, you'll pull your chest onto the kayak. Your paddle will help keep you balanced as you do this, as long as it stays perpendicular to your kayak. You can then hook a foot over the paddle shaft to get a bit more support for the next step. Now, turn your body towards the stern of your kayak and swing your legs into the cockpit. Then, twist your body around and slide back into the seat, keeping your center of gravity low and your weight on the paddle float side of the kayak the whole time.

Now that you're settled back in the cockpit, you'll have a lot of water to contend with, so you'll either have to head to shore or start pumping it out.

ROLLING A KAYAK

One of the greatest things about kayaking is that, as a sport, it has something to offer everyone. For many, kayaking is simply a means of getting some exercise in the outdoors, but for a growing number of people, kayaking provides the excitement of almost continuously learning new skills and refining techniques, adding the satisfaction of making progress over time. For this latter group, there are some great reasons to take the time to learn to roll, and I can assure you that it will be worth your effort.

For whitewater kayakers, rolling is an important skill to master. Knowing how to roll doesn't mean that you shouldn't expect to swim every once in a while, because sometimes you won't have a choice. But swimming should be one of

your last resorts. Aside from being tiring, frightening, and humbling, swimming makes you much more vulnerable to hazards. A reliable roll is also a great confidence-builder; you'll be more relaxed on the water and more inclined to try new things. Invariably, this results in a steeper learning curve.

Although rolling isn't an essential skill for any kayaker, there's no question that a reliable roll is a huge asset as it lets you paddle more safely and helps you be more relaxed on the water. You'll find your increased confidence will support you in exploring new elements of the sport.

These are some pretty compelling reasons to learn to roll, and the fact that you're reading this probably means that you're interested in doing so. Are there any

limitations on learning to roll? Unless you're allergic to getting your head wet, you'll be happy to hear that that any reasonably fit paddler can learn to roll, because rolling relies on good technique, not power. But there are some limitations on which kayaks can be rolled. As a general rule, the only kayaks designed for rolling are sea/touring kayaks and whitewater kayaks.

In this segment we're going to take a quick look at how the roll works, so you know what's involved. If you're keen to learn to roll, I highly recommend taking a rolling clinic from a good paddling school. I also wrote a book and DVD (both called *Rolling a Kayak*), available in book stores and outdoor stores everywhere, that deal exclusively with rolling techniques.

Did You Know?

The kayak roll comes in a number of forms. In fact, taking into account all of the Greenland kayak roll variations, there are over 100 types of rolls. Practically though, most paddlers only need to consider one roll; the one that will get them upright!

The C-to-C and Sweep Rolls

The two most basic rolling methods are the C-to-C and sweep rolls. Both of these rolls are great for beginners, but there is much debate among kayak instructors as to the better technique for new kayakers. In my opinion, there's no correct answer to this question. I've taught both techniques extensively and have found that different people take to different techniques more quickly—it's almost completely arbitrary. In some cases, I've even started out teaching one type of roll and after watching a kayaker struggle with it, switched techniques with great success.

The idea behind these rolls (and all other rolls for that matter) is simple. To roll a kayak upright from the upside-down position, you're going to extend your body out to the side and get yourself as close to the surface of the water as possible. From this position, your paddle will act like a brace and provide the support needed to hip snap your kayak upright.

The hip snap (or hip flick) refers to the action of rotating your hips to right your kayak; it is without a doubt the single

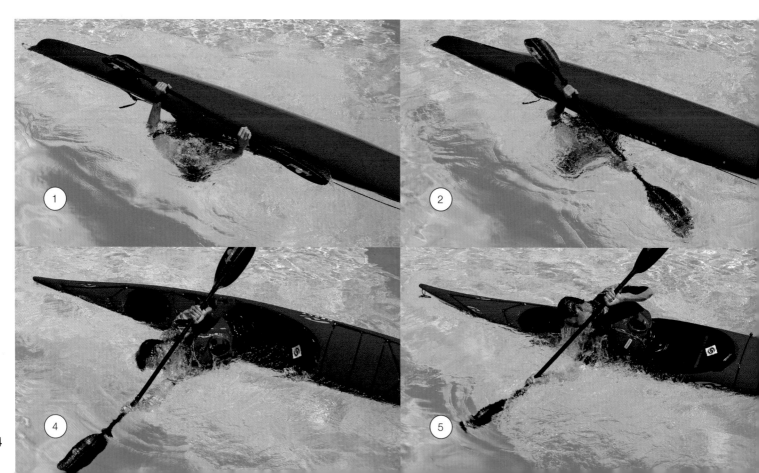

most important technique to master for success with your roll. Although we didn't call it the hip snap, we already looked at the technique in the Braces segment of this book. The idea behind the hip snap is fairly simple. By staying loose at your waist (applying the first Golden Rule by separating your upper and lower body movements), you can use your knee to roll your hips and right your kayak while your head and body remain in the water. To do so effectively, you'll need some form of support for your upper body. For most rolls, your paddle provides this support. For a hand roll, your hands provide the support. The fact that your hands can provide enough support against the water to roll your kayak is a testament to how important the hip snap is for the roll.

As your hips roll your kayak upright and under your body, your head, upper body, and lower body work together to finish the roll. This is where the bracing technique we looked at earlier comes in, and where I'll again emphasize the importance of dropping your head towards the water. By dropping your head to the water, you allow your bottom knee to continue to pull your kayak upright. At the same time, dropping your head keeps your center of gravity low while your body moves over your kayak. If you lift your head instead, you'll pull on your top knee, which will effectively pull your kayak back upsidedown.

Dropping the head towards the water is extremely counterintuitive—but I'll also restate that it's absolutely essential! Your head should be the last part of your body to come back up.

The sweep roll in action. Notice how the hips have rolled the boat almost completely upright before the head comes out of the water.

CHAPTER SEVEN

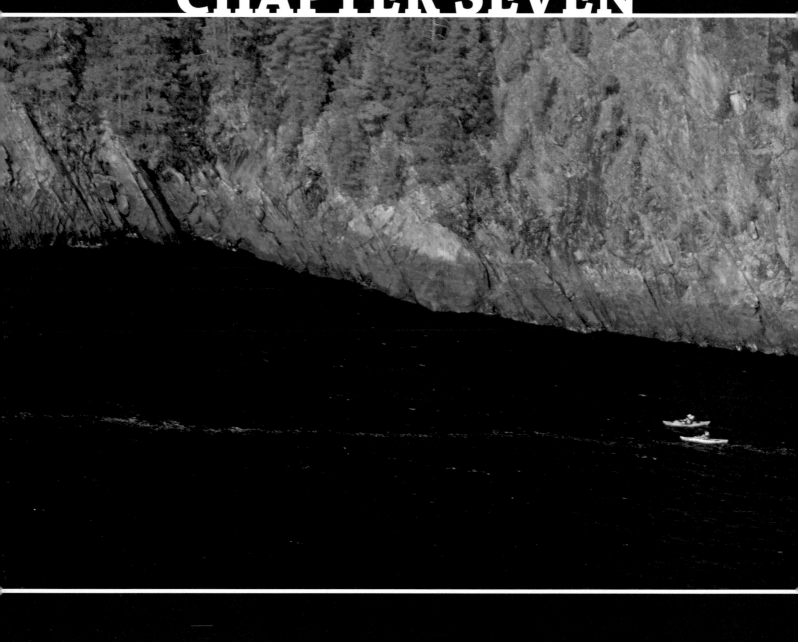

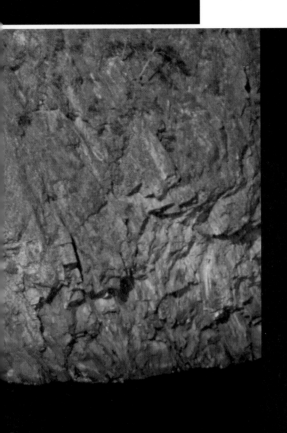

PADDLING IN EXPOSED CONDITIONS

EXPOSED WATER
EQUIPMENT CONSIDERATIONS

DEALING WITH WIND

TIDES AND TIDAL CURRENT

EXPOSED WATER SAFETY

As we said from the start, the line between recreational kayaking (which doesn't require specific training or instruction) and sea kayaking is basically drawn by your exposure to wind and waves and your proximity to shore. As soon as you venture into water that isn't protected from wind and waves, and/or you travel further from shore than you can comfortably swim, you are entering a new world. You need to protect yourself by getting informed and developing practical rescue skills. It's a challenge well worth tackling! The skills and knowledge you'll gain from a sea kayaking course will provide a huge boost in confidence and open a road to self-discovery that remarkably few people in this world are ever fortunate enough to travel.

This chapter offers some of the basic information related to dealing with the major variables (some would call hazards) that you might encounter in exposed water. Please understand that this is not designed to replace professional instruction, but to give people interested in venturing into exposed water a knowledge base, and to act as a refresher for those people who have already taken instruction. The reason I stress this is not because exposed water paddling needs to be a high risk activity. It doesn't! The problem is that if something goes wrong, an exposed water environment is one of the most unforgiving places. When things go wrong, they can go very wrong, very quickly! For that reason, if you're going to venture onto the ocean or into a big body of water, it is highly recommended that you take a sea kayaking rescue course.

EXPOSED WATER EQUIPMENT CONSIDERATIONS

If you're going to travel on open water, the equipment you decide to bring along will be less driven by preference and more driven by necessity—for safety's sake. Of course, every trip is different, so you'll need to decide what gear makes the most sense. The nice thing about kayaks is that there usually isn't any lack of storage space, so if you think there's even a small chance that you could use something, you might as well bring it.

SEAWORTHY KAYAKS

First of all, not every kayak is seaworthy for exposed water conditions. In particular, recreational sit-inside kayaks are inappropriate unless they have secure bulkheads and hatches with watertight compartments in both the bow and stern. These watertight compartments prevent the kayak from completely swamping (and potentially sinking) in the event of a capsize. They also make it much easier to perform any of the capsize recovery techniques, because your boat will be floating higher in the water.

SAFETY GEAR AND ACCESSORIES

Spare Paddle

Although the chance of it happening in open water is low, imagine your predicament if you break or lose a paddle! Always carry a spare paddle in your group. Your spare paddle should be a two-piece break-down paddle, placed in your kayak's storage compartment or stored securely under the stern deck bungees.

Water and Snack

If you were driving a powerboat on open water, you'd certainly make sure to bring enough gas to get you home. That's exactly why you need to bring plenty of water and snacks—to keep your body fueled.

Bilge Pump

If you're paddling a sit-inside kayak, you'll need a pump to empty it out if it gets swamped. It's usually a good idea to have a couple of hand pumps, which can be shared within a group.

First Aid Kit

A waterproof first aid kit should always accompany you. A good way to waterproof your kit is to use a Pelican case or an empty Nalgene bottle.

Emergency Kit

If you're ever get caught out in a storm or in conditions that don't make traveling home safe, an emergency kit is designed to make an unplanned night out bearable, if not comfortable. An emergency kit can be a twenty-liter dry bag with some warm, dry clothes, raincoat and pants, headlamp, matches, fire starter, snacks and even a small tarp and rope. Many accidents happen because of the decision to continue due to unwillingness or inability to spend a night out.

Navigation Tools

Navigation tools ensure that you always know where you are and where you are going. These include guidebooks, charts, compass, tide and current tables, GPS units, and a watch.

Paddle Float

A paddle float is a good piece of self-rescue gear to bring along, but only if you are trained and practiced in its use.

Tow line

A tow line gives you the option to offer a hurt, seasick, or exhausted paddling buddy a helping hand.

Communication Devices

A key element to staying safe on the water is maintaining a form of contact. The cell phone is the most common communication device, but if you're not sure it will work in the area you'll be traveling, use either a marine VHF radio (which requires training) or a satellite phone.

Signaling Devices

Signaling tools let you catch someone's attention if you're in need of help. The most common signaling tools are whistles, flares, smoke canisters, strobes, and mirrors.

DEALING WITH WIND

The direction of the wind in relation to where you're traveling can have all sorts of different effects on your kayak. Obviously, a headwind will slow you right down. In fact, as a general rule, for every additional five knots of headwind, you can expect to be slowed down by half a knot. A twenty-knot headwind will slow you down by two full knots. Since an average paddler's speed is around two and a half to three knots, your actually progress would be cut down to less than one knot! The only good thing about paddling into a headwind is that it usually means you're paddling directly into waves, which is the easiest way to deal with waves because you can see them coming and they don't tend to knock your boat off course.

Paddling with a tailwind is a different story altogether. The same general rule regarding the effects of wind applies—meaning that for every five knots of tailwind, you can expect to travel half a knot faster. Throw some waves into the equation and you'll cruise along even faster than that. In fact, the right waves will let you surf your way downwind without taking any strokes at all. On the same token, wind waves will also make traveling downwind more challenging because you can't easily see them coming. Over time and with experience you'll develop a general paddling awareness which will let you confidently paddle in

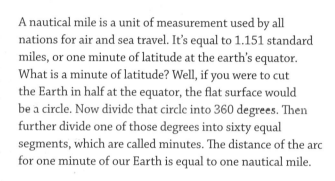

A tailwind can really give you a boost. Not only will it help push you along, but you can often surf the waves as well.

these conditions. Until then, you can expect to feel a little uneasy with your back to the wind and waves. In fact, some people will even get seasick when paddling with their backs to the waves as their boat pitches forward and back unpredictably.

The trickiest wind conditions for paddling are beam (side) winds. Not only will you usually have to deal with waves coming at you from the side, but your kayak will want to turn into the wind, or weathercock (as discussed in Chapter 4). That's where a rudder or skeg will come in really handy, as they prevent the stern of the kayak from getting pushed by the wind, which turns the bow upwind. If you don't have a rudder or skeg, you have a few other options which we discuss in the Going Straight Forward segment of Chapter 5.

The trickiest wind conditions to deal with are when the wind and waves are coming from an angle behind and to the side of your kayak. In this case, instead of paddling directly to your end destination, you're usually better off paddling directly downwind and then turning ninety degrees to paddle to your end destination perpendicular to the wind. This means paddling further overall, but your travel will be much easier this way.

Did You Know?

Most areas have somewhat predictable winds, although you can never be certain what the wind is going to do. If you're new to an area, take the time to learn the common wind patterns and choose your trips accordingly. For example, you might find that in the area you intend to paddle, the wind always seems to pick up around midday, and then dies down in the evening. This probably means that a morning paddle is your best choice.

TIDES AND TIDAL CURRENT

The rise and fall of tides and the subsequent tidal currents work on a predictable schedule, based on the twenty-eight-day lunar cycle. The schedule is different for every area, and can be predicted quite accurately using regional tide or current atlases.

In some areas, such as the Southern United States, the tidal variance is generally very small and in some cases inconsequential. In other areas, such as around Great Britain and Canada, tides can change the sea's level by over twenty-five feet in some spots, and help create massive tidal rapids with bus-sized waves and whirlpools that can swallow a tree.

If you're paddling in an area affected by tides and known to have tidal currents, it obviously has to play into your paddling plans. You might consult your local tide charts and decide to only paddle during slack tide, which is the relatively calm time between changing tides. Of course, the prudent thing to do is take a sea kayaking course in which they'll teach you how to make plans around tides and tidal currents.

In areas with large tidal variations, powerful tidal currents and rapids can be formed such as those of Reversing Falls in Saint John, New Brunswick.

EXPOSED WATER SAFETY

As we already mentioned, with a little common sense, paddling in exposed water doesn't have to be a dangerous activity. The problem is that you're in a dynamic environment, which can throw a curve ball at you once in a while. To minimize the risk and to put yourself into the best position to deal with the issues that arise, there are a few things to know.

First off, it's worth talking about the idea of paddling alone in exposed conditions. The truth of the matter is that there are people out there who paddle alone in highly exposed conditions. This definitely doesn't mean that it's a wise thing to do: quite the opposite! I highly suggest that you never paddle alone in exposed water. As I just mentioned, the problem

with dynamic water environments is that they aren't totally predictable. Things can happen that are totally out of your control, and if you're in exposed water and don't have a helping hand available, you could find yourself in a disastrous situation.

It's important when in exposed water to always paddle with another competent kayaker.

GROUP DYNAMICS

Paddling with a group of people is the safest way to travel in exposed conditions—assuming everyone's on the same wavelength. It's essential to realize that the group is only as strong as the weakest paddler. It's also important that you understand and appreciate the reasons the other people in your group are paddling. You might be out there for a workout, but the others in your group might be there to catch a glimpse of a bald eagle or other wildlife. In a case like this, you're either going to have to accept and accommodate the others, or decide to paddle with a different group.

SIGNALS

When paddling in exposed conditions, paddle and whistle signals can come in really handy. Not only can your group get spread out very quickly, but wind will often make communicating by voice impossible. Of course, signals are only useful if everyone in your group knows how to interpret them, so it's worth going over them before heading out on the water. Here are some of the most basic and universal signals.

Whistle

- A single whistle blast is used to draw attention.
- Three short, sharp whistle blasts are used to indicate an emergency.

Paddle

- A paddle held vertically into the air is used to communicate "go ahead".
- A paddle held horizontally into the air is used to communicate "stop".

TOWING

There may come a time when your paddling buddy needs a little helping hand and a tow might be in order. This could involve towing a friend who is swimming or towing an empty boat. In some cases, this could involve towing a friend in the kayak.

In the Swimming section of the previous chapter, we looked at the situations in which towing a swimmer or gear makes sense, as well as the different options for doing so. Basically, if it's closer and easier to tow someone and/or their gear to shore instead of trying to do a reentry on the water, then you might as well do so. For short tows to shore, the same towing techniques will work with all types of kayaks, whether you're on a river, the ocean, or a lake.

Towing someone in their kayak requires a different technique, which will come in handy if you ever have to deal with an injured, seasick, or exhausted paddler in open water. The most basic and most common means of towing someone is using a technique called the "in-line tow". The in-line tow involves clipping your tow line onto the bow of the boat that you're going to tow. For long distances, you'll want to use a long tow line thirty to forty-five feet (or nine to fourteen meters) to avoid having the kayaks banging into each other. The tow line should be attached to your body by a quick release belt that you can pop off at a moment's notice should the need arise.

Did You Know?

Some PFDs have a quick-release harness system. The chest harness is secured around the center of the PFD and should tighten independently of the straps that secure the PFD to you (i.e. the tightness of the PFD should not rely on the chest harness). The harness has an easy quick-release system up front. The tow line is attached to a steel O-ring on the back of the harness. These systems are great, especially since you don't have to worry about forgetting to bring your tow line. With that said, a simple quick-release tow belt will work just as well, if not better. Since the tow line will be anchored lower down on your waist, your upper body will be jerked less each time the tow line is pulled taut.

EXPOSED WATER HAZARDS

Aside from the obvious hazards of wind and waves, and the risks associated with paddling further from shore than you can comfortably swim, there are a few other dangers worth mentioning.

First off, when you're paddling on exposed water, weather should always be a major concern of yours. Weather can (and will) blow in quickly, and although clouds and rain don't present a danger on their own, wind, lightning and fog can be dangerous. During storms, the wind can be intense, quickly drumming up large waves. Battling strong winds and waves is not what most people in their right minds would call fun.

Lightning should also be a major concern when you're paddling on open water. When you're out there, you'll be the highest point for a quite a distance in any direction, which makes you an ideal lightning rod. It's a bad idea to get caught out in a lightning storm, so at the first hint of thunder, get off the water as quickly as possible.

Fog can also have a real impact on your safety—for obvious reasons. When you're on open water, it's easy to lose your sense of direction in fog because you have very little visual reference for your location. If it's windy, you may be able to maintain a course based on waves. Otherwise, if there's any chance of fog, you should have a chart and compass—and know how to use them. Even better, stay close to shore so you can just turn around and follow the shoreline back home. The other advantage of staying close to shore is that you won't have to worry about other boat traffic, which is the next biggest hazard for open-water paddlers—whether you're paddling in foggy or clear conditions. In some areas, boat traffic will be next to nonexistent, but in a busy harbor or on a crowded lake, there can be a lot of people enjoying their time on the water. As a general rule, if a boat is bigger and faster than you, it has the right of way. This doesn't represent the actual "rules of the road" for boat traffic, but it does represent a common-sense set of rules paddlers should live by. The biggest water-traffic hazards don't actually come from the biggest boats. In fact, bigger boats are very predictable. They stay in the deep water and don't make any aggressive maneuvers. The biggest issue when dealing with these boats involves staying out of their way and being prepared for

Weather can roll in quickly and if you're caught in an exposed area, you'll likely find yourself battling wind and waves—at a minimum.

the large waves caused by their wakes. The best way to deal with these waves is to simply point your boat directly into them. The boats you should be most wary of are sail-boats, small powerboats (like the ones used for waterskiing) and personal motorized watercraft. These boats will maneuver unpredictably and the people steering them will often be distracted: they may not notice you until it's too late. The best way to avoid all other boat traffic is to stay close to shore and avoid paddling during the twilight hours, when you'll be hardest to see.

Big boats are much more predictable than small craft, but you'll need to watch out for large waves caused by their wakes.

Did You Know?

Whenever you go paddling it's important to create a float plan and to make sure you give it to someone who is not going to be on the water with you. For day outings, this simply means telling someone where you're going paddling and when you expect to be back. If there's no one around to tell, make sure you leave a note that says more than "Gone paddling. See you soon."

GETTING LOST

As you can imagine, getting lost on the water isn't any fun. In many cases, avoiding getting lost is as simple as following a shoreline, so you can just turn around and follow the same shoreline home. Throw a bunch of islands and some long crossings into the equation and you're opening the door to navigation woes. If you plan on entering a more complicated marine environment, you absolutely need to get trained in navigation techniques. This includes training in the use of a chart and compass, GPS, and tide and current tables if they're relevant to your area. These are all topics that go beyond what we're able to cover in this book, although there are some good references available on the market. The best idea is to take a sea kayak navigation course.

CHAPTER EIGHT

PADDLING IN SURF ZONES

CHOOSING A BEACH

PADDLING IN SURF

If you have a fun little surf zone near you, then you have my envy. Although I'm fortunate enough to have some of the world's best lake, river and whitewater paddling in my backyard, I have to travel a long way to find a surf zone. But the travel is worth it! Surf zones really are natural wonders!

In this chapter, we're going to start by looking at the difference between a friendly and dangerous surf zone, and then finish with the basics of paddling in a surf zone.

CHOOSING A BEACH

Surf zones are funny. Some surf zones can be considered the most entertaining natural playgrounds ever, while other surf zones are as close in character to a playground as a toxic waste dump. With that said...

First off, you should know that surf waves are formed when ocean swell hits shallower sections of water. If the transition to shallower water is abrupt, as it often is with an offshore reef, the waves will grow quickly and then dump hard. If the transition to shallow water is gradual, the waves will rise slowly and break with less ferocity. You can probably see why

the safer surf zone involves a nice sandy beach with a long gradual slope. It also makes a huge difference if this surf zone is not subject to the direct impact of an ocean's swell. Somewhere in between the beach and the great wide ocean, there is a reef, shoal, or island(s) to absorb some of the energy of the ocean swell as it rolls into shore.

A less obvious consideration in dictating the "safety factor" of a surf zone is the presence of riptides. A riptide is formed because the nature of some beaches allows waves to force more and more water up the beach and trap it there.

This trapped water is now higher than ocean level and it's desperately looking for a way to get back down. Once it finds an opening back out to sea (usually a deeper channel in the surf zone), all that trapped water rushes towards it forming a riptide. Riptides can result in very powerful currents traveling directly out to sea. Experienced surfers sometimes use rip currents as conveyor belts to get out past the choppy shore break, but unprepared swimmers can get caught in rip currents and swept out to sea—a dangerous situation to find yourself in. Since rip currents are usually fairly narrow channels of current traveling directly out to sea, the best way to escape their grasp is to swim parallel to shore. As you can probably imagine, swimmers who don't understand the nature of rip currents often try swimming directly back to shore, which means they're only fighting the current—a battle they are almost guaranteed to lose.

Most rip currents are well known by the locals, and surf zones with riptides are usually marked as such by signs. Of course, if you don't know the area in which you're going to be paddling, it's only prudent to ask someone who does.

KAYAKS FOR SURF ZONES

A wide range of kayaks work well in surf zones. In fact, it's probably easier to identify the kayaks that aren't good in surf zones. The only kayaks you shouldn't bring into surf zones are recreational sit-inside kayaks. The problem with these boats is that the first big wave you encounter will swamp your kayak and then probably flip you. Then you're stuck with a heavy, swamped boat in the midst of breaking waves. Not only is this a pain in the butt to deal with, but it's a real hazard to you and to anyone else who's using the beach. Whitewater kayaks, sea kayaks (with the use of a skirt), and sit-on-top kayaks all work great. Of course, unless you're experienced and know how to roll a kayak, you're much better off using a sit-on-top kayak, because it's way more stable and won't swamp if you end up flipping: you can just climb back on top of it and keep going.

photo by Lisa Utronki

You'll also find surf kayaks and wave skis, which are specifically designed for playing in surf. The biggest difference between these boats and other kayaks is the hull design. Surf kayaks and wave skis are designed for speed and carving ability while surfing a wave. Wave skis are different from surf kayaks in that they have no deck. They're basically the sit-on-top version of a surf kayak, although they don't give up anything with regards to performance. Both are fast and fun, but highly responsive, so you need to be a competent paddler in order to take advantage of them.

PADDLING IN SURF

Regardless of which type of kayak you use, there are three main challenges when paddling in surf: launching, landing, and surfing.

Launching in surf can be pretty tricky because waves will be constantly washing up the beach and knocking your gear around. If you're paddling a sit-on-top kayak, you're in luck! The easiest thing is to drag your kayak into a foot or two of water, wait until a wave passes and then hop onto your boat and start paddling out. If you're using a higher performance sit-inside kayak (whitewater, sea or surf kayak), it's not going to be so easy. If you try, even if you do have the balance to slide into your kayak while it's floating (which is very difficult) you almost assuredly won't have time to get your skirt on; the first wave that hits you will swamp your kayak. The best place to get into your kayak is on the beach, in a spot where one of the bigger waves will wash

When launching, hold the bow of your kayak directly into the waves. As soon as you get a calm moment, hop in and start paddling.

enough water up its slope to lift you off the sand and let you paddle out. Take a minute to watch the shore break before picking your spot. When you decide the time has come, make sure to align your boat directly into the oncoming waves. Climb in and get your skirt on as quickly as possible. If you're using a sea kayak, slide your paddle under the deck lines so that it doesn't get washed away. You'll probably have to push yourself out with your hands.

Once you've launched and you're on the move, the best way to get through waves is to keep your boat pointed directly into

To punch a breaking wave, paddle hard directly at it, keep your weight forward, and plant a powerful last stroke to pull yourself through. It also helps to tuck your head behind your top arm to shield your face from the wall of water.

them. If the wave is breaking, you'll probably want to take a few hard strokes and hit the wave with some speed in order to break through it.

Surfing waves is one of the coolest feelings imaginable, and if you have the gumption to launch in a surf zone in the first place, you're probably interested in giving it a whirl. The first thing to know is that if you're going to try surfing, you have to expect to flip—repeatedly! The trick to surfing is to line yourself up with the direction of the wave, facing the shore. As the wave gets close to your stern, take three or four hard forward strokes to bring yourself up to full speed when the wave starts picking up your stern. At this point, gravity starts to come into play; if you've timed your strokes correctly, and if the wave is steep enough, you'll be able to stop paddling and start surfing. To control your surf, you'll use a stern rudder (see Chapter 4). If you're using a shorter kayak, your stern rudder can offer a lot of turning power while you're surfing. On the other hand, a long boat (such as a sea kayak) tends to have a mind of its own. Once it decides to turn in a particular direction, it's almost impossible to stop it.

The author demonstrates exactly why you should take your time and wait for a set of waves to pass before trying to land.

Even in tiny surf you need to hop right out of your boat and pull your kayak out of the waves.

The author gets ready to hop out of his kayak and drag his boat out of the surf zone.

Landing in surf is a lot more difficult than paddling out. Remember that waves come in sets and there are often spots along the beach where waves are less powerful, so take the time to watch and learn the rhythm and pattern of the waves as they roll in before making your move.

Once you make your move to shore, you have two choices. You can surf a wave into shore, or you can chase a wave into shore. Chasing a wave means following on the heels of the last wave in a set. By chasing a wave you don't need to worry about controlling a front surf and losing control of your kayak. With experience, you'll likely end up using a combination of the two by surfing the wave into shore until a point just before it starts breaking. You'll then slam on the brakes with some aggressive back strokes and then chase that same wave right into shore. Either way, the key to staying upright is staying square to the waves.

Once you reach shore, don't relax too quickly. Your boat will get beaten around by the shore break unless you hop out, grab the bow, and drag it up the beach. The more loaded your kayak is with gear, the more careful you'll have to be. Not only will a heavier boat be harder to control, but if it does get away from you it can really hurt you or someone else.

As a general rule, if you're going to enter a surf zone, expect to swim. To prepare for swimming, make sure nothing is sitting loose on the deck of your kayak. It's also important to consider the other beach users in this regard. A runaway kayak can pack a wallop! Make sure that you're not paddling in a busy swimming area.

CHAPTER NINE

RIVER RUNNING

BASIC CURRENT DYNAMICS

EQUIPMENT CONSIDERATIONS

SHUTTLES

PADDLING IN CURRENT

Rivers provide some of the most fantastic kayaking experiences. There's something really satisfying about starting in one place and finishing in another. There's also something very cool about using a river's current to make your way downstream. With all the beautiful rivers in the world, there are endless opportunities for kayakers, but a lack of understanding about—and the subsequent fear of—moving water, has limited the number of kayakers taking advantage of these natural playgrounds. This chapter is designed to remove some of the unknowns and open the doors to some wonderful new paddling possibilities.

First off, since many rivers have flowing water, it's important that we clearly draw the line between what we're going to call "river running" and what should be considered whitewater kayaking. The most obvious difference relates to the type of rapids, if any, that are involved. For the river running that we're considering, the current involved will create (at very most!) small, straightforward and wide-open rapids that feature little waves and which can be swum with little risk of injury. This refers to only Class 1 and light Class 2 rapids on the international classification system.

RIVER CLASSIFICATION

Whitewater is rated on a scale of increasing difficulty from Class 1 to Class 6. This classification system provides a useful guide to the technical difficulty of a river, but there are so many other variables that can have a huge impact on the difficulty or danger of a river. Is the water warm or freezing? How remote is the run and how far away is help? Can you walk out if you need to, or is the river in a canyon? Are the rapids long and continuous or short and separated by calm pools? As you can see, there can be massive differences between two rivers of the same class. For this reason, it's your responsibility to find out more about any river you're thinking of paddling. For many areas, there are guidebooks with detailed descriptions and images of the rivers, and more of these are available each year. It's always a good idea to pick up a guidebook. You can also ask questions on online chat boards or stop in at the local outdoor retailer for information. You can never be too well informed.

The classification system is still very useful for giving a river a general level of difficulty. It must be accepted that this system is in no way an exact science and that it's open to interpretation. Here are some general guidelines for the whitewater classification system.

Class 1 (Easy)

Fast-moving current with small waves and few obstructions that are easily avoided. Low risk. Easy self-rescue.

Class 2 (Novice)

Straightforward rapids with wide-open channels that are evident without scouting. Occasional maneuvering is required. Competent paddlers will easily avoid any rocks or medium-sized waves. Swimmers are seldom injured.

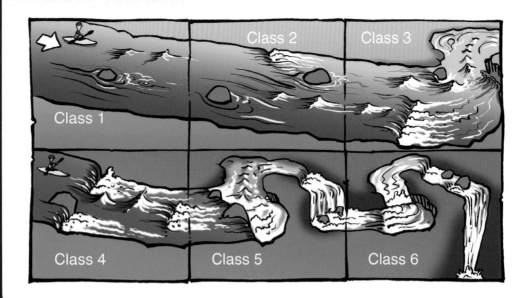

Class 3 (Intermediate)

Rapids with moderate, irregular waves, strong eddies and currents. Complex maneuvers and good boat control are required. Major hazards are easily avoided. Scouting is recommended for inexperienced paddlers. Self-rescue is usually easy and injuries to swimmers are rare.

Class 4 (Advanced)

Powerful, turbulent, and predictable rapids with large, unavoidable waves and holes or constricted passages. Fast and reliable eddy turns and precise boat handling are needed to navigate safely through. Scouting is necessary, and rapids may require "must make" moves above dangerous hazards. Strong Eskimo roll highly recommended, as there is a moderate to high risk of injury to swimmers. Self-rescue is difficult, so skilled group assistance often needed.

Class 5 (Expert)

Extremely long, obstructed, or violent rapids with exposure to substantial risk. Expect large, unavoidable waves and holes, or steep, congested chutes. Eddies may be small, turbulent, difficult to reach, or nonexistent. Reliable Eskimo roll, proper equipment, extensive experience, high level of fitness and practiced rescue skills essential for survival. Scouting highly recommended, but may be difficult. Swims are very dangerous and rescues are difficult.

Class 6 (Extreme)

These runs exemplify the boundaries of difficulty, unpredictability and danger, and have almost never been attempted, if ever. The consequences of errors are very severe and rescue may be impossible. Only expert teams with ideal conditions and extensive safety systems should ever consider these rapids.

Another main differentiator between recreational river running and whitewater kayaking has to do with the type of kayak you're using. Although whitewater kayaks provide a huge performance advantage over recreational kayaks, the trade-off is that they aren't as stable, and if you do flip, you won't immediately fall out of the kayak. That means you'll actually spend time upside down in your whitewater kayak, which makes putting on a helmet and getting training absolutely essential before paddling down even the slowest and smallest of rapids.

The last major difference between recreational river running and whitewater kayaking goes right back to our original description of recreational paddling. As long as you stay close enough to shore so you can always comfortably swim there and get help, then it can be considered recreational kayaking. But if the river you're interested in running takes you into a canyon, deep into the wilderness, or anywhere else that would make walking out to get help impossible or anything more than a real inconvenience, then it probably shouldn't be considered recreational kayaking and you should seriously consider getting professional instruction.

Now that we've more clearly (although certainly not conclusively) identified the limits of what should be considered recreational river running, the rest of this chapter will try to give you a base of information from which you should be able to better identify hazards and make better decisions. With this said, and despite the fact that I'm a real advocate of recreational river running, you need to appreciate that even the mellowest current has an amazing amount of power and can exert amazing pressure on objects in its path. Make no mistake, moving water has the potential of being lethal, so a conservative attitude is always prudent, as is seeking out professional instruction. If you plan to paddle a section of river, be sure to thoroughly investigate everything downstream from your put-in. Changes in elevation, sharp corners, or constricted channels all dramatically increase the speed and power of even the smallest river. Likewise, if another river joins the stream that you're paddling, expect water volume to increase and the effects of current to become more powerful.

If you flip while paddling a recreational kayak, you'll simply fall out of the boat and spend next to no time upside down.

Two paddlers hang out in an eddy while another plays in a breaking wave.

BASIC CURRENT DYNAMICS

Water in motion is also very similar to fire; it carries tremendous energy. Although we can roughly forecast how it will act, it is incredibly dynamic and anything but predictable. It's also one of the most captivating and stimulating natural wonders. Just as you can spend hours on end watching the dancing flames and listening to the crackling of a campfire, it's easy to get lost watching and listening to water as it cascades down a creek or flows under a bridge. But the magic of each hides a terrific power. In fact, moving water is the single most powerful and destructive force on the planet, and this can't be ignored even when you're paddling on what seems to be a peaceful, slow-moving river. You need to appreciate that even very light current and shallow water can exert amazing pressure on objects in the path.

Simplified, a flowing river has current and eddies. The current is the water moving downstream. Usually there's a main channel, but a midstream rock or an island can divide the main current and form multiple channels that all have current. An eddy is a pocket of water directly downstream from some form of obstruction for example, a rock or a part of the riverbank that juts out. The deflection of water by the obstruction creates a relatively calm area below—a paddler's parking spot. The concept is quite simple. When water is deflected by an object, it's pushed away from one area and towards another, creating a differential in the amount of water between the two areas. Because of gravity, the river naturally wants to equalize this differential by flattening itself out. To achieve this effect, the water circles back into the area from which it was originally deflected. The result is an eddy on the downstream side of the obstruction. This flow creates an upstream current (from bottom to top) in the eddy that can vary in strength from being almost unnoticeable (on gentle, slow rivers) to very powerful (on fast-flowing, big-volume rivers). An eddy line forms where the upstream-flowing water of the eddy (the eddy current) meets the downstream-flowing water of the river (the main current), creating a helical (whirlpool-like) flow that's usually fairly easily distinguishable as a rough line. The eddy line is narrowest and most crisply defined at the top of the eddy and dissipates toward the bottom of the eddy.

Something else to consider is that water in motion carries incredible momentum. One of the results of this momentum is that when a river bends, a lot of water gets pushed to the outside of the turn, where it's then deflected in the right direction. This is very important for a kayaker to understand because it means that if you were to float down the middle of a flowing river, you would get taken to the outside of a bend, along with most of the river's water. This is where the current is fastest and the waves the biggest. This is also where debris such as fallen trees (very real hazards) will end up. On the inside of a bend, the water will be flowing much more slowly. Obviously, knowing this impacts how you navigate down a flowing river. It doesn't mean that you'll always want to hug the inside of a corner, but it certainly means that it's a good default course to take.

BASIC RIVER TERMINOLOGY

Upstream/Downstream

Pretty straightforward—upstream is where the flow is coming from and downstream is where it is going. In other words, the net flow of water is from upstream to downstream. This does not change!

River Right/Left

These directions refer to the corresponding side of the river when looking downstream. They are the most frequently used indicators.

An inflatable kayak is one of the best boats for dealing with current.

The rescuer tosses a throw bag to a swimmer.

EQUIPMENT CONSIDERATIONS

In most cases, any recreational kayak will do the trick for paddling on rivers, but if you have some real current and waves to contend with, there are a few things you might consider. When dealing with Class 1 and 2 , sit-on-top hard shell or inflatable kayaks are the best for the job because they're super-stable and they won't swamp. You might also want to invest in a spare, break-apart paddle that you can stow on top or inside your kayak in case you break the one you're using. A throw rope is another good idea. A throw rope/bag is a bag with one end of a rope attached, the rest of the rope coiled inside, and the other end of the rope free. The throw rope is designed to make carrying the rope more convenient and throwing the rope more accurate. To use it, you hold the free end of the rope in one hand and throw the bag with the other. As the bag travels through the air, the rope uncoils from it until it reaches its end (which is tied to the bag.) Throw ropes are the primary safety tools used in swift-water rescues because they allow someone on shore to accurately throw a rope to someone who needs help in the water. A last piece of equipment that you should probably consider is a helmet. Because the river current will be carrying you faster than you normally travel, any collision will have more impact. Although most people think helmets are only for protecting kayakers from rocks when they're upside down, the helmet is actually just as useful for protecting yourself from other paddlers' boats and paddles.

SHUTTLES

River running is unique from other types of paddling because sometimes it requires traveling from a point A to a point B, particularly if you have current to contend with. A shuttle refers to the way you prepare for such a trip, so things are as easy as possible when you arrive at the end point of your trip (the takeout). Trust me when I say that after a day of paddling, you'll really appreciate a well-organized shuttle.

Although there's no single way to organize a shuttle, one rule that's consistent is that before you start out on the river you'll want to get as many vehicles down to the takeout as possible. If your vehicle isn't going to be one of those, you want to make sure you have everything you'll need at the takeout in one of the vehicles that will be there.

I usually bring a small pack with the things that I want for the takeout, like a change of clothes, a towel, and a drink. If my vehicle isn't going to be left at the takeout, I can just throw that pack into a vehicle that will be.

If you have a group with multiple vehicles, you have a few choices. The best option is to unload all the people and gear at the put-in and then drive all the vehicles to the takeout. One vehicle will bring all the drivers back to the put-in. Of course, before running this shuttle, make sure that everyone knows which vehicles are going to stay at the takeout, and give people a chance to place the personal stuff they want at the takeout in one of those vehicles. If on the way to the put-in you have to pass by the takeout, you might be better

Did You Know?

One of the biggest and most common shuttle mistakes involves leaving the keys for the takeout vehicles at the put-in. Trust me when I say that you DO NOT want to be the one to make this mistake! Within our circle of friends, doing so results in a hefty beer fine and endless abuse from the others. If you're leaving your vehicle at the takeout, you have two options. You can carry the keys in a secure pocket (which won't open if you swim), or you can hide the keys somewhere on your vehicle. Either way, be sure to let the others in your group know where those keys are.

off stopping at the takeout to drop off one or more vehicles along with all the personal gear you want to have at the end. Then, you can consolidate everyone and the gear into the remaining vehicles heading up to the put-in. This is a particularly useful shuttling technique if the distance between the put-in and takeout is significant.

Of course, you don't always need multiple vehicles to run a shuttle. Depending on the distance, you could actually run/jog the shuttle, or bike the shuttle. I would still recommend doing so before hitting the water, so your vehicle and personal gear are waiting for you at the take-out.

In some cases, the only shuttle option is to hike up the river and paddle back to your car.

TAKEOUT HERO

One of my best takeout memories comes from paddling with my buddy Paul on a creek in British Columbia, Canada. Our friend Pam offered to come along, drop us off at the put-in and then meet us at the takeout a few hours later. We were only expecting to be on the water for a few hours, but the creek became a tricky canyon with very difficult whitewater. Already two hours late, we gave up our mission and started hiking out of the canyon—hauling our boats behind us by rope. Another hour later (three hours late for the takeout), we made it to the dirt road that connected the put-in and takeout. With darkness quickly approaching, we got ourselves ready for a long night out in the bush. Then we saw headlights coming around the corner and Pam pulled up.. We were exhausted, cold, and feeling terrible for putting Pam through the worry and wait. Pam popped the trunk and exposed a bag of nacho chips, jar of salsa, and a couple of cold beers. The dark cloud that hung over us was quickly blown away.

After a long day outside, some simple pleasures can make the takeout experience something you look forward to, rather than a necessary evil. A cooler with ice-cold drinks and some snacks will make you a hero, as will some extra warm, dry clothing for that person in your group who forgets to leave their gear in the takeout vehicle.

PADDLING IN CURRENT

Paddling in current can be one of the greatest feelings, so don't be surprised if you soon want to explore whitewater kayaking. As I mentioned at the beginning of this chapter, for the purposes of recreational kayaking, we're only considering Class I—at most Class 2—rapids. But even light current is incredibly powerful, so it's worth looking at some of the basic techniques and concepts for dealing with it.

As a general rule, your goal when paddling through current is to spend the least amount of time on eddy lines. Sometimes you can just point your boat downstream or upstream and paddle, staying in the main current and avoiding eddy lines all together. Keeping your boat straight and your body forward, you can paddle through some pretty big waves this way. Other times though, it will be desirable to work your way in and out of eddies and use the current to help you get where you want to go.

CROSSING EDDY LINES

Crossing an eddy line into or out of an eddy is called an eddy turn. If you can do a solid low or high brace lean turn on flat water, then you've already got the individual skills you'll need to do an eddy turn. It's simply a matter of combining timing, edging and your lean turn together with the right plan of action.

The first thing to know is that when crossing into the main current from an eddy, you always want to cross the eddy line with your boat on about a forty five-degree angle pointing upstream or up current. It is very important that you carry some forward speed into this maneuver, because you want to cut across the eddy line decisively and not end up stranded in the confused water between the two currents.

As soon as your bow crosses the eddy line, the main current will grab it and pull it downstream or with the current. If you're not prepared for it, it can flip your boat. The way to prepare is to tilt your boat downstream—edge it on the downstream side—as you cross the eddy line, in the direction of your turn, just as you'd edge your skis to carve a turn or lean a motorcycle into a corner.

As you cross the eddy line with some speed and edge your boat downstream, keep your paddle at the ready in the low brace or high brace position on the downstream side of your kayak.

Recognize the low brace lean turn that you practiced on flat water? Using this technique, you should be able to perform a smooth turn either into an eddy or into the main current so you can continue downstream. When you are heading downstream and crossing the eddy line from the main current to the eddy current, the only difference is that your stern will of course be pointing upstream; but you'll still cross the eddy line with speed, on about a forty-five-degree angle, and edge your boat on the downstream side.

The timing of the transition from edge to edge is critical for smooth entries and exits from current—especially in fast-moving current—and with a little

To turn out of an eddy, approach the eddy line at a forty-five-degree angle with forward speed.

As you cross the eddy line, edge your boat downstream and have your paddle ready to low brace on the downstream side.

With your boat held on edge, it will carve a turn downstream.

Ferrying is a technique used to cross current laterally.

FERRYING

The ability to use current to help you get where you need to go will transform your ability to maneuver in moving water. The most basic means of doing so is called a ferry.

Ferrying is a technique used to cross current laterally. It's accomplished by paddling with your kayak angled upstream, so that during your crossing, you make enough upstream progress to counteract the speed at which the current is pulling you downstream. In milder current, you can point yourself more directly across to your destination, but when the current gets stronger, you'll have to keep a fairly aggressive upstream angle on your kayak to fight the current that will otherwise pull you downstream. If the current is strong and there are waves to contend with, you'll also need to keep your boat tilted on a slight downstream angle throughout your ferry. This ensures that water doesn't pile up on the upstream edge of your kayak and flip your boat.

If you're starting your ferry from an eddy, you'll want to cross the eddy line like you did for an eddy turn, but with a bit more upstream angle, so your bow doesn't get pulled downstream. As you cross the eddy line, you may need a few sweep strokes on the downstream side of your boat to keep your bow pointed upstream.

SCOUTING

The difference between kayaking in current and many other sports, like mountain biking or skiing, is that you can't always just put on the brakes and stop to take a look at what's going on ahead of you. This is why scouting is so important. Although Class 1 and 2 whitewater will usually be very wide open and straightforward, you can't afford to make any assumptions about what lies below if you can't see it, because you may not be able to stop. Scouting is the action of looking ahead at a rapid to identify any hazards and decide on a route. You can scout either from your kayak ("boat scouting") or the riverbank. Of course, scouting from shore is generally the best means, because you can get a variety of perspectives and a clearer view of the rapid as a whole. On the other hand, when dealing with Class 1 and 2 whitewater, boat scouting will often suffice because the river should be wide open and easy to see.

As I mentioned earlier in this chapter, if you plan to paddle a new section of river, be sure to thoroughly investigate everything downstream from your put-in. Pay special attention to drops in the riverbed, sharp corners, or constricted channels; all dramatically increase the speed and power of even the smallest river. Likewise, if another river joins the stream that you're paddling, expect water volume to increase and the effects of current to become more powerful.

HANDLING ROCKS

When dealing with Class 1 and 2 currents, the chances are quite low that you'll encounter rocks, but it's important to know what to do if the situation does arise. When being carried towards a rock in current, your best option is obviously to turn and paddle (ferry) away from it; but if it can't be avoided, you need to take actions that will probably fight your natural instincts. The natural response to colliding with a rock is to turn sideways and lean away from it, which puts your kayak between yourself and the rock. Unfortunately, this action has very undesirable results, as leaning away from the rock means leaning upstream. As soon as your kayak hits the rock, current will pile up on your upstream edge and flip you mercilessly. You now find yourself upside down against a rock. So—what should you have done?

When drifting into a rock that can't be avoided, you need to keep your boat tilted downstream to prevent your upstream edge from catching the main current. In lighter current, or when dealing with lower-angle, rounded rocks, this might simply mean holding an edge and bouncing into the rock or its pillow at the ready with a brace. You might even have to push yourself laterally off the rock with your downstream hand. In faster current, or when the rock is more vertical, you may need to lean your whole body into the rock while holding your boat on edge. You may also need to push yourself laterally off the rock with your downstream hand quite aggressively. Of course every situation is different, but the key is always to keep your upstream edge from catching water. Lean into the rock and give it a big (but gentle) hug!

Rocks just below the surface can also wreak havoc on unsuspecting paddlers and are common causes of broken paddles. With experience, there's no reason to get caught by surprise by such a rock, as your river reading skills will allow you to recognize them early on. If your path does take you over a submerged rock, you should try to hit the rock as straight on as possible, with enough speed to drive over the top of it. This is a good reason to keep your kayak fairly straight with the current in the early learning stages—before your river reading skills have developed. Of course, this is also why using a plastic kayak for river running is a smart choice. The last rocks we're going to consider are those under the water that can have a real "impact" on an upside-down paddler. This is only an issue for paddlers using sea or whitewater kayaks, which paddlers won't simply fall out of as they flip upside down. Fortunately, these are the most seldom-encountered rocks. In fact, even most whitewater paddlers will never make the acquaintance of an underwater rock. In the event that you do meet a rock underwater, there are a few things you need to keep in mind in order to minimize the impact. Of course, your first line of defense is to roll up as quickly as possible. The less time you spend underwater, the better. If that isn't an option, you need to look at other ways to stay protected. Your most protected position while upside down is tucked forward against your kayak. Your helmet (which you're be wearing if you're paddling in a situation where flipping is a possibility) and life jacket will take the brunt of any impact with rock. That's why you learn to move to this protected position when setting up for rolls or doing a wet exit.

If you find yourself sideways against a rock, lean into it and keep your boat tilted downstream. You can then push yourself laterally off the rock.

RESCUES

Swimming

There are two ways of swimming through a rapid. You can swim defensively or offensively. Defensive swimming is also referred to as "body surfing" and involves floating downstream in a protected position: lying on your back, feet downstream, arms out to the side and with your whole body floating as close to the surface as possible. This is the best swimming position to assume if your goal is to ride out a rapid, or if you're in shallow water and worried about hitting rocks.

If you need to actually get somewhere, you'll adopt the offensive swimming technique. Offensive swimming involves getting on your stomach and swimming hard with the front crawl.

The defensive swimming, or "body surfing" position.

Offensive swimming in current.

Towing

If someone in your group ends up going for a swim in current, the easiest way to help them out is to give them a tow to shore. While you're doing that, hopefully there's someone else around to gather the gear. If there are only two of you, and the swimmer is fine and happy, you may want to gather the gear and let the swimmer swim their way to shore.

The easiest way to tow someone is to give them the stern of your kayak to hold onto. If the swimmer is agile enough, and the current calm enough, they might be best off to climb onto the stern of your kayak and hang onto your waist. Just keep in mind that the last thing you want to do in any rescue situation is turn the rescuer into a victim. If there's any doubt about the rescuer's ability to safely tow the swimmer to shore, you will probably all be better off letting swimmers swim themselves to shore.

HAZARDS

Stationary obstacles in moving water are always potential hazards. While rocks and fallen trees can make navigating difficult, strainers are downright dangerous. A strainer is any obstacle that allows water to pass through, but not boats or people. The most common form of strainer is created by boulder sieves, logjams, fallen trees, or dense bush and trees by the banks of a river in flood. Strainers are so dangerous because moving water can sweep you into the impassable obstruction and the force of the current can hold you pinned in place. If your head is trapped underwater and you are unable to swim to safety, a rescuer will have only seconds to complete a successful rescue.

Foot entrapment is another serious hazard. Many riverbeds consist of a jumble of rocks and other debris. When wading in moving water, should your foot go into a depression or crack, the current can push you off balance, trapping your foot in place. Once again, the force of moving water can make it extremely difficult or even impossible to extricate yourself from this dangerous predicament. The safest strategy for avoiding foot entrapment is to always swim when in moving water above knee level. This will mean crawling those last few steps into shore instead of standing up, but a little bump on the knee is better than the possible alternative.

Lastly, avoid all weirs and low head dams like the plague! The hydraulics created at the bottom of these man-made structures can be deceptively powerful and will often make it impossible for a swimmer to escape.

A strainer lets water through, but stops bigger objects... like you!

CHAPTER TEN

KAYAKING FOR EVERYONE

SEA KAYAKING

WHITEWATER KAYAKING

KAYAK FISHING

KAYAKING FOR FITNESS

PADDLING WITH KIDS

SNORKELING AND DIVING FROM A KAYAK

KAYAK CAMPING

LEAVE ONLY FOOTPRINTS

One of the greatest things about kayaking is that it really is for everyone! It's a fantastic reason to get outside, spend time with friends and family, or get some exercise. Kayaks are even great vehicles for taking part in other activities, like snorkeling or fishing.

Up to now, this book has talked about kayaking in fairly general terms, but in this section we're going to look more closely at specific kayaking activities with the hopes of introducing you to some new ones.

SEA KAYAKING

Sea kayaking is a natural progression from recreational kayaking. In fact, as a recreational kayaker, there's a good chance that you're already using a sea/touring kayak. The only reason you aren't "sea kayaking" yet is because you don't have the training that will allow you to confidently and safely explore more remote marine environments, or travel further from shore than you could comfortably swim. If you aren't using a sea kayak right now, you will probably find that they are a little more tippy than the boat you're used to. You might also find that you feel a little uneasy sitting in a small cockpit with your legs tucked under the thigh hooks, but I assure you that will pass quickly—especially after you do your first wet exit, which I highly recommend doing right away. Once you get over any initial trepidation, you'll quickly come to appreciate your new-found speed and edge control. It's like hopping into a Ferrari after driving an SUV!

Why would you want to become a sea kayaker? There are lots of reasons to want to become a sea kayaker. Many people (myself included) find the key to staying enthused about anything is the opportunity to learn and improve. Sea kayaking provides the chance to do both on a grand scale. The marine environment is one of the most dynamic and diverse on the earth. You can spend a lifetime exploring and still discover new and exciting things on a regular basis. There are also endless ways of challenging yourself, if that's what interests you. On the flip side, the knowledge gained through taking sea kayaking courses may not change where and how you paddle at all. For many people, the confidence gained from sea kayaking courses is more than reward enough. Not only will it make your time on the water more relaxed and enjoyable; it will let you safely bring new paddlers onto the water to share the experience.

One of the greatest things about sea kayaking is that it allows you to discover places you would probably never otherwise know existed.

So what do you really learn from a sea kayaking course? That's a tough question! It's like asking what you would learn from a golf pro—it really depends on where your weaknesses are and how much training you already have. What I can tell you is that the ultimate goal of a sea kayaking course is to develop your paddling proficiency and your rescue skills, your understanding of the marine environment and its hazards, your navigation skills, and your ability to make sound decisions both off and on the water so you minimize the chance of getting caught in a compromising situation.

WHITEWATER KAYAKING

To become a whitewater kayaker, you need a good attitude, a healthy appetite for fun, and the willingness to get your head wet. Too many people hear the term whitewater kayaking and immediately dismiss the idea of trying it out because of preconceived notions of what the sport is all about. It's impossible to blame anyone for that when every time you turn on the TV or flip through a magazine, you see some kayaker defying death by plunging off a massive waterfall. For most people, that's what whitewater kayaking is! The truth of the matter is that equating whitewater kayaking with that image of a paddler dropping over a sixty foot waterfall is like equating hiking with a climb up Everest. It's important that we dispel this myth as quickly as possible, because it has kept far too many people (young and old) from experiencing the thrill of whitewater kayaking. The bottom line is that whitewater kayaking can be as mellow and relaxed or as adrenaline charged as you want it to be. Although there are inherent dangers involved with the sport (as there are with all sports), it will probably surprise you to hear that whitewater kayaking is one of the safer outdoor adventure activities. In fact, there are far fewer whitewater kayaking injuries than there are mountain biking or downhill skiing injuries. With that said, the fact that you're playing in moving water means that mishaps have the potential of becoming very serious. This is why it's important that you take a whitewater kayaking course and learn the basics from an expert instructor.

There has never been a better time to take a whitewater kayaking course. Just as mountain biking evolved with the advent of front and rear wheel suspension, and skiing evolved with the development of parabolic and fat skis, over the past decade, whitewater paddling has gone through a massive evolution. As the sport gained popularity through the mid '90s, manufacturers competed aggressively with each other. The result has been kayaks that offer new paddlers a steep and forgiving learning curve, as well as kayaks that provide expert paddlers the opportunity to push the sport to new levels.

If you're interested in trying whitewater kayaking, there are a large number of resources that can help you get your feet wet. Your best option is to contact your local paddling shop or outdoors store. There's a good chance that they'll offer introductory courses—often in heated pools over the wintertime too! They'll also be able to point you to the best

local kayak schools or paddling clubs. Another great option is to ask those who are already part of the whitewater community—and these people are easy to find, thanks to the Internet. At Boatertalk.com you'll find thousands of whitewater paddlers from around North America who will be more than happy to give you their two cents. World Kayak is a relatively new organization whose primary goal is to help new paddlers get into the sport. They host regular events across North America and have a highly informative and interactive website (worldkayak.com) that's well worth checking out.

Contrary to popular belief, whitewater kayaking is not just reserved for the adrenaline junkie.

KAYAK FISHING

The idea of fishing from a kayak is a relatively new idea to many people, which is ironic when you consider that the kayak was developed by the Inuit as a hunting and fishing boat. But more and more people are realizing that kayaks are great for fishing. In fact, kayak fishing is currently one of the fastest growing sports in North America. Paddlers are going fishing, anglers are going paddling, and it's amazing to see the size of fish that are being caught from kayaks. Believe it or not, there are anglers out there who are routinely pulling in hundred-pound-plus fish from their kayaks. During these fights, the kayak angler will often get taken on what's called a sleigh ride, where they get towed over long distances. Of course, this isn't indicative of why most people are getting into the sport. Fishing kayaks have really boomed in popularity because of their advantages over motorized boats. First off, they are very inexpensive to buy,

maintain, and especially to run, when you consider the cost of gas these days. Kayaks are also much more durable, easier to transport, highly maneuverable, and capable of getting into shallow, rocky, and weed-choked waters—which makes new fishing areas accessible. Of course, there are also the great environmental and health benefits associated with using a human-powered boat instead of one that's gas-powered. Last, but certainly not least, is the fact that fishing from a kayak brings you closer to the water and to the world below the surface. As your boat glides stealthily through the water, you will undoubtedly find yourself more in tune with those wily critters beneath you.

Although it is possible to fish from any type of kayak, sit-on-tops have become the favorite for most anglers because

they provide the most versatility when it comes to fishing position. You can sit sideways with your legs over the side of the boat, as if you were on a dock. Some models even let you stand up. Of course, another bonus is the fact that you can reenter them from the water if you happen to fall out. With this said, both sit-on-tops and sit-insides work great for fishing. In fact, manufacturers have responded to the growing demand by offering "angler editions" of some of their kayaks with fishing-specific features such as rod holders, paddle clips, live-bait wells, holding tanks and even camouflage color schemes.

If you're interested in learning to fish from a kayak, check out *The Ultimate Guide to Kayak Fishing* book by Scott Null and Joel McBride. There are also kayak fishing guide services in some areas. The great thing about kayak fishing, though, is that all you need is a valid fishing license, a safety-conscious attitude and the desire to try something new.

KAYAKING FOR FITNESS

As more and more people realize how user-friendly and fun kayaks can be, a whole new crowd has switched on to kayaking as means of reaching their general fitness goals (losing weight and building strength). It's easy to see why! Nearly everyone in North America has a lake, river, or ocean within easy reach, and when you compare going for a paddle with working out in a gym, few people would argue about which one's more fun. Many people are making the complete switch to kayaking for fitness because it offers a full body workout, and it's a great option for people plagued with lower body injuries sustained from activities like running. Others are integrating kayaking into their current fitness programs because of its effectiveness in developing core and upper body strength. The importance of core strength as the foundation of total fitness has received a lot more press in recent years. Strong muscles in your abdominal core give you better posture, slim your waistline, and support you physically in every activity from simple everyday movement to running marathons, which also means fewer injuries.

If you use the right equipment and correct technique, and if you paddle on safe waterways, another appealing thing about kayaking is that it poses little risk of injury or accident while still delivering satisfaction and results. Unlike running, kayaking is low-impact—there is no hard pounding to cause muscle and joint damage. Unlike cycling, there is no chance of high speed crashes and what cyclists call "road rash"—scraped skin with embedded dirt from the road. Kayaking can be used for fitness at all levels and for all ages, from seniors interested in a low-impact sport to younger, elite athletes interested in serious competition. Kayaking races are becoming more popular, with many short, long-distance and marathon-style races to choose from. Also, multisport adventure races, usually a combination of kayaking, mountain biking, trekking and climbing, are ever-increasing in popularity. For those who already participate in these thrilling events, paddling is often the weakest individual element, so time invested specifically in kayak training can bring about the greatest overall improvement in race results.

If you're interested in learning how to use kayaking as a fitness activity, it's worth picking up the new book by Jodi Bigelow, *Kayaking for Fitness*. The book takes readers through an eight-week fitness program, with separate tracks for beginner, intermediate and expert paddlers.

PADDLING WITH KIDS by Eugene Buchanan

Rarely will you find a better craft for getting your kids out on the water than the rec kayak, whose wide, flat bottom makes it stable enough for even the most torrential tantrum. Clad with a properly fitted PFD (a must any time they're on the water) children of all walks can use rec kayaks for a seamless indoctrination into the wonderful world of paddling.

Like kids themselves, such family-friendly kayaks come in all shapes and sizes. There are two types that are best for tykes: sit-on-tops, where you and your child sit on top of a depression in the boat's hull; and sit-insides, which have large, open cockpits for ease of entry and exit. With no claustrophobic cockpits to cram into, both types let you and your kids paddle away on the first try without fear of tipping, and both are perfect for paddling as a family, whether your child is still in Pampers or on her way to a Ph.D.

If you're planning on paddling and parenting where water and air temperatures are warm, sit-on-tops make the perfect choice. Your entire bodies are out in the open, and your child can even jump in the water to cool off and then climb back aboard. Self-bailing holes near the seat keep the water out, and in the rare event of a capsize, you can simply flip it over and climb back aboard.

Sit-insides have the same wide, stable bottom, only they also come with an enlarged cockpit. This keeps you and your brood out of the elements better than a sit-on-top, and keeps water from puddling around your derriere. Most single-cockpit rec kayaks are big enough for you and your child, and some come with cockpits so large they can fit your mother-in-law as well (though that might be too close for comfort).

When your kids get older, you can position them in the front of a two-person craft while you steer from the stern (and provide the lion's share of the power). Some parents even store gear in front of smaller children's feet so they won't slide under the deck, and others use a dry bag or pad as a booster seat, having their kids straddle it like riding a pony. The added height helps both their paddles and their heads clear the sides of the boat.

No matter which design you go with, sit-on-top or sit-inside, the learning curve to each is akin to riding a tricycle. There's no learning, no leaning, and most importantly, no rolling. Simply hop on and go.

Both styles are available in one, two and even three-person models, meaning that, like the family station wagon, you can position your kids wherever you want. In the early years, you're best putting your child directly in front of you (bring an extra lifejacket for them to sit on). Then they can grab the paddle between your hands and feel the motion of propelling it forward. Don't expect to win any speed records as it inhibits your paddling motion, but do expect it to open your child's eyes to the wonders of watersports.

Whatever type and size you get, base your decision on where you'll use the craft most. If you think your kids will like it, get a tandem that you can take them out in during their impressionable years, that you and your spouse can use whenever the opportunity presents itself, and that even your kids can use together as soon as they're old enough.

A few rules of thumb before heading out: always make sure your kids are wearing a properly fitted PFD when out on the water. Until they're capable swimmers and mature enough to handle a capsize, stay close to shore (let your child's age and ability determine your route selection). And tell your kids what to do beforehand in event of a capsize. All this will make them—and you—better prepared for any unannounced visits to Atlantis.

Finally, when it comes to paddles, don't get them sized for Yao Ming. Adult paddles are usually too big for children to use, so go with a child-specific model. You can also find child-sized canoe paddles that, even though you're in a kayak, can instill the lesson of locomotion. Teach them the proper paddling technique by having their hands shoulder width apart (a lot of kids put them too close together), and show them how to rotate the torso with each stroke.

Then head out and have fun. Today's family kayaks are more stable than a household on a school morning, so there's no reason not to get your feet wet in this wonderful sport.

Eugene Buchanan is the former publisher of Paddler *magazine and author of the forthcoming book* Getting Outdoors with your Kids.

SNORKELING AND DIVING FROM A KAYAK

When we talk about using a kayak as a vehicle for other activities, snorkeling and diving are the perfect examples. Sit-on-top kayaks are great platforms for doing both, as they easily carry all the required gear. Some boats even have wells molded in, specifically designed for carrying an air tank. Sit-on-tops are also very easy to re-enter from the water and provide excellent stability when climbing aboard. In fact, sit-on-tops act a lot like floating docks. For snorkeling, a common approach is to use an ankle tether that attaches a leash from your leg to the kayak. The leash allows you to cruise around as you please, with your boat trailing along behind like a faithful hound. Your boat will also act as a marker to let other boat traffic know you're there, and it gives you the option of taking a break and hanging out on the side of your boat for a rest. The only thing to know if you're doing this is that you'll want to swim somewhat into the wind, so that your boat doesn't get blown into you and become a nuisance.

KAYAK CAMPING

Like canoes, kayaks are great vehicles for camping because they can carry a lot of gear and get you to campsites that may otherwise be totally inaccessible. In particular, kayaks excel at reaching remote ocean beaches or islands in open or unsheltered water. On the other hand, canoes excel on trips that involve portaging because your gear will be placed in the canoe in backpacks which can be carried at the same time as the canoe. Because of the narrow hatch openings and smaller storage spaces in a kayak, gear needs to be packed into the kayak in small pieces. If you need to portage, you either have to carry your boat with all the gear inside, which will be extremely heavy and impractical unless you use a kayak cart. Even then, pulling a fully loaded kayak on a kayak cart will be very difficult on anything but a smooth trail. The only other options are to unpack all your gear and carry it in small pieces or repack it into a backpack—both of which are a real pain in the butt.

The best kayaks for camping trips are large sit-insides that have separate, waterproof compartments accessed through hatches. These hatches help keep your gear dry (although you never want to rely on them being 100 percent watertight) and prevent gear from

scattering or being lost in case you flip. Sit-on-tops can work as well, although you'll need deck bungees for securing dry bags. The downside is that your food is not nearly as protected from the sun, and a mountain of gear will allow the wind to push you around a lot more.

When packing your boat, there are a few things to keep in mind, because the distribution of your gear within the kayak can have a big effect on the handling of

Did You Know?

Label all your dry bags clearly with pieces of duct tape. There's nothing more frustrating than having to open all your dry bags to find out where you put something like your headlamp. You can also get dry bags made from a see-through material.

your boat. As a general rule, you'll want to pack the heaviest items at the bottom of the boat and as close to the centerline as possible. Keeping the weight low will make your boat more stable; having heavy items on the deck of the kayak will make it more unstable. Since you can't expect your waterproof compartments to actually be waterproof, you should pack anything that shouldn't bet wet into small dry bags. Obviously, all your clothing and sleeping gear should be in dry bags, as well as any food that needs to stay dry. Wrapping stuff in a couple of heavy-duty garbage bags can do the trick, but dry bags are the surest way to keep it all safe from getting wet. The dry bag is the camper's best friend and it comes in all shapes and sizes. In general, twenty-liter dry bags are great for fitting into kayaks, although it's nice to have some smaller ones to fill the spaces between bigger bags.

Something else to consider when packing your boat is which gear you'll need to get at first. Those things should be the last pieces that you pack. For example, the last few things that I'll pack into the boat might be the day's lunch and the utensils I'll need, along with a warm fleece and toque that I can just throw on when I get off the water.

Of course, one of the easiest ways to make a camping trip a prized memory for those in your group is to have good food. This doesn't mean that you need an exotic menu, but it does mean that you should offer some variety in food (pasta with tomato sauce gets a little tiring after eating it for three meals straight!). Creating a camp menu can be difficult, so if you're new to it, it's well worth picking up one of the many books on the topic. They offer some great tips and great recipes. In particular, check out *Camp Cooking: The Black Feather Guide*, as well as *The Paddling Chef*

Did You Know?

It doesn't take much to keep the smiles on everyone's faces during a camping trip. On the flip side, it doesn't take much to turn those frowns upside down. The key to keeping campers happy is making sure everyone is warm and fed, so keep some extra warm gear, water and snacks available and within easy reach.

LEAVE ONLY FOOTPRINTS

This segment evolved in a funny sort of way. It all started with a piece I was writing about the appropriate way to relieve yourself in the outdoors. When I originally wrote this segment, it was in the Paddler's First Aid chapter, because there have been more than a few times on the water when I needed to go so badly that it felt like a medical emergency! But it didn't take me long to realize that the topic was part of a greater issue relating to how to enjoy the outdoors while minimizing your impact upon it. This whole idea of "leaving only footprints" is an important concept for anyone who enjoys the outdoors.

Let's start by looking at the very topic that kick-started this section. What is the etiquette for relieving yourself in the outdoors? Different areas have different rules for relieving oneself. With good planning you shouldn't have to worry about where to drop number two, but if you do have to, solids should never go directly into the water. They should be deposited far away from the water in catholes dug into the active layer of soil. Having said that, on some high-traffic rivers you are required to carry all solid waste out. As distasteful as it sounds, it's really not a big deal if you have the right system, and there are a

few companies, like Restop, with great products for the purpose.

The Restop system provides a really easy and clean system for carrying out your solid waste.

As for going number one, in ocean environments you're best off urinating directly into the water. The rules for relieving yourself in freshwater environments can differ depending on the region you're in. For example, the Colorado River sees a lot of boat and camping traffic, and so you are asked to urinate directly into the river. Otherwise, campsites would quickly begin smelling foul. In greener and wetter environments, it may be the accepted practice to relieve yourself in active soil, well away from the water. The bottom line is that you need to be aware of the rules for the area you're paddling in.

Another big factor that relates to leaving only footprints is how you deal with wildlife. Although the visual impact of respecting wildlife will be unnoticeable, the real impact is significant. For the wildlife, there's nothing good about interactions with humans. Put yourself in the animal's shoes for a moment. You live in the wild and are in constant search of food for survival. You're getting into the months when food is harder to come by. You finally find a source of food and then a group of humans in kayaks shows up and starts moving towards you, pointing and taking pictures. As hungry as you are, you have no choice but to flee. On the other hand, maybe you've watched enough humans come and go to realize that they aren't a real threat. In fact, they can even be a great source of food. Little do you know that becoming "friendly" with the humans will likely result in your destruction at the hands of a hunter, or by wildlife control persons who have no choice but to consider you a "problem" animal.

Of course, these are two very simple examples of how interactions between humans and wildlife can end badly for the wildlife. The point is, their lives are tricky enough without us complicating things, so keep your distance and do your best not to disturb them. For these same reasons, it's also important that you never feed wildlife, purposefully—or inadvertently by storing your food improperly.

SHIT FLOWS DOWNSTREAM

As the saying goes, "shit flows downstream". For paddlers this is more than just a saying, it's a fact. As a paddler, you can expect to come across garbage on your travels. It's easy to tell yourself that this isn't your junk, but why not take a moment to grab it and save the next paddler the experience of paddling by the garbage. It's not like your kayak doesn't have the space!

A curious beluga whale approaches.

but I will let you know of the impact campfires can have on the environment, and how you can minimize it.

There are two main reasons for avoiding campfires. For one, the appearance of many areas has been degraded by the overuse of campfires—not only due to the scarring of the ground, but from the cutting of trees and tree limbs due to the demand for firewood. Secondly, campfires open the doors to the major

Did You Know?

If there isn't a fire ring, the best option is to use a fire pan or box. These folding metal boxes contain your fire and ashes so that you don't leave any fire scar on the ground.

Another topic worth discussing is how to minimize your impact on the environment while on kayak camping trips. Your ultimate goal should, in fact, be to leave only footprints. With that goal in mind, we're going to talk quickly about dealing with waste and campfires.

We already talked about how to deal with human waste. Now we're going to talk about how to deal with all your other garbage. You shouldn't have very much garbage if you've done a good job of planning ahead to ensure accurate menu quantities and to minimize packaging. There are two good ways to deal with food waste and garbage that you generate—or that you might unfortunately find along

your travels: you can either pack it out, or you can burn it over a hot fire (if it can be done safely). Although burying your food waste is often the most convenient thing to do, it's not a good option because animals will smell it and dig it up. Animals that get used to scavenging human food usually become a real problem.

A lot of people couldn't really imagine camping without a campfire—which is totally understandable. There is something very special about sitting around a campfire in the great outdoors and reveling in its warmth while watching the light dance across the faces of the other campers. Having said that, I can't comfortably tell you not to build campfires, environmental disaster we know as forest fires.

If you're going to build a fire, here's how to minimize its impact. First off, use existing fire rings, keep your fire small, and allow the wood to burn completely to ash. If you're going to a well-used campsite, don't expect readily available firewood around camp. Since cutting branches around camp (even dead ones) is a bad option, make some stops before reaching camp to collect dead and fallen branches and driftwood. When it comes time to leave camp, if you're using a fire pit, make sure that all the wood is completely burned and then douse it with water to put it out. If you're using a fire pan or box, burn the wood completely, soak the ashes to cool them and then either pack them out as garbage (which is required in many river corridors) or scatter the remains over a large area, well away from the camp.

Fortunately, environmental awareness and education have been improving over the past decade, but it will be an ongoing battle. The absolute best way to make a difference is to lead by example. The next time you're camping with a group, take the initiative and establish some environmentally conscious ground rules that your group will follow.

THE UNSUSPECTING FOREST FIRE FIGHTER

It was the summer of 1991, and my job was "safety kayaker" for raft trips on the Ottawa River. I was ahead of the trip when I came around a corner and saw smoke rising from the trees ahead. All of a sudden, one of the small trees on shore burst into flame. I couldn't believe my eyes. The forest along the banks of the Ottawa River was on fire, and I was watching it happen. I raced to the shore and started splashing the flaming tree with my paddle. Fortunately, it wasn't large enough to catch the others around it on fire and the fire quickly died, but smoke still rose a bit deeper into the forest. I hopped out of my kayak and immediately discovered the source. It was a hastily constructed and unattended fire pit built on a bed of pine needles. Using my helmet, I dumped water from the river onto it and the fire pit hissed menacingly back at me. As I continued to dump water on the fire pit, the raft trip came around the corner and I called them over. Their massive bailing buckets would do a much better job. The first raft landed and threw me their bailing bucket. As I carried the full bucket to the fire pit, water sloshed out of it and onto the ground. Moments later, I was shocked to hear that same menacing hiss from below my feet, more than ten feet from the fire pit. I dumped more water in the area and the hissing intensified. It didn't take long for me to realize that the whole root system under the surface bed of pine needles was glowing red-hot, which was why that small tree along the shore had burst into flame. The whole forest in that area was a time bomb. For the next hour, we scrambled and dumped bucket after bucket of water over an area about thirty feet in diameter. Finally, the hissing stopped and the local fire department arrived and took over. We all learned a pretty important lesson that day.

CHAPTER ELEVEN

PADDLER'S FIRST AID

BLISTERS

REPETITIVE MOTION DISORDERS

BACK PAIN

SHOULDER DISLOCATION

HYPOTHERMIA

HEAT STROKE

JELLYFISH STINGS

STINGRAY STINGS

One of the greatest things about kayaking is that major injuries are very uncommon because, unlike outdoor sports such as mountain biking and downhill skiing, if you "fall" while kayaking, you splash in the water rather than slamming onto the ground. Most paddling-related injuries stem from overuse or a lack of protection from weather conditions.

In this chapter, we're going to take a quick look at the most common paddling injuries and how to prevent and/or treat them.

BLISTERS

Although some people would scoff at the idea of a blister being considered an injury, blisters can be incredibly debilitating. The most common paddling blisters are caused by the paddle and appear on the inside edge of the thumb. The biggest thumb knuckle in particular tends to take the brunt of the paddle's punishment and blisters are often accompanied by tenderness because there really isn't much in the way of natural padding on this part of your thumb.

Blisters are very predictable, so you might as well take preventative steps from the start. The best way to avoid blisters is with some type of barrier between your skin and the paddle. Moleskin works great for this, as do light paddling gloves. In a pinch, duct tape will also do the trick.

Treating a blister simply involves protecting it from any further irritation. Once again, this means using moleskin, gloves or duct tape, although you'll want to have a nonstick surface against the blister itself, otherwise you'll just tear the skin off. One of the best ways to protect a blister is by cutting a hole in a piece of moleskin to create a "donut" that surrounds the blister. Large blisters can be drained of their fluid with a sterilized needle and then covered with antibiotic ointment and a bandage.

REPETITIVE MOTION DISORDERS

Repetitive motion disorders (RMDs) are self explanatory—they're injuries caused by overuse over a period of time—sometimes a few days, sometimes months. The most common to paddlers is carpal tunnel syndrome (a wrist affliction) and tendonitis in the arm. It is worth noting that tendonitis in the lower body isn't unheard of—usually the result of poor outfitting.

There are a few ways to avoid developing RMDs. First off, pace yourself and keep a loose grip on your paddle. Don't wait until your body rebels before deciding to call it quits. At that point, the damage is done. This probably means going for very short paddles in the early stages. Secondly, if you're prone to overuse injuries, you can make some gear decisions to minimize the wear and tear on your body. In particular, use a paddle with minimal offset (feather), which requires less wrist rotation. Furthermore,

you'll want to use a flexible and light paddle—with more importance going to its flexibility. I mention this because carbon fiber paddles are the lightest paddles on the market, but they're also the stiffest paddles available. A stiff paddle doesn't absorb as much energy. You'll get a more powerful stroke, but your arms will absorb all the shock associated with paddling, contributing to repetitive motion disorders. Plastic or fiberglass paddles (or a combination) provide a good mix of flexibility and light weight.

Treating RMDs is fairly straightforward, and is best remembered with the acronym RICE: Rest, Ice, Compression, Elevation. You really need to rest the associated joints, apply ice and some light compression, and raise the body part to reduce swelling. Anti-inflammatory drugs can also help reduce the pain and swelling.

Did You Know?

Ice or cold packs are best used as quickly as possible following an activity, because they'll be most effective in reducing swelling and killing the pain at that time. They should be applied for no more than 15 minutes at a time, several times a day, and they should never be applied directly to the skin. Try wrapping the pack with a light towel and then use a tensor bandage to hold it securely in place.

BACK PAIN

Anyone who suffers from back pain will tell you how painful and debilitating it is. There are so many possible reasons for experiencing back pain; it's impossible for us to consider all of them here. If you are experiencing any type of back pain, you have no choice but to visit a doctor right away. There are a few things that we know contribute towards some types of back pain, and which you should be aware of as a paddler.

For some people, the sitting position in a kayak can induce back discomfort. There are a few common causes of this. Tightness in the hips and legs (especially the hamstrings) makes sitting with your legs in front of you more difficult. If you're not a flexible person, you should consider a recreational kayak that allows your legs to assume a more flexed position. The higher your knees are, the less strain there will be on your hamstrings. This might mean avoiding sea kayaks, as they offer less leg room than most recreational kayaks. The outfitting in your kayak will also have a huge impact on your comfort: we looked closely at this in Chapter 2. In general though, a good back band/support is important, as is having some type of support under your thighs. It's also worth noting that your back support and your PFD should work in unison. If your kayak has a high back support (which can really help), a standard PFD could position flotation in the lower back, getting between you and your back support. PFDs that have all the flotation moved away from the lower back are readily available.

SHOULDER DISLOCATION

For recreational kayaking purposes there really is no reason to experience a shoulder dislocation. It's when you get into more advanced kayaking that the shoulder dislocation becomes a more serious and real concern. In particular, it comes into play when you start paddling in conditions that force you to use your braces or to roll. Obviously, this means that whitewater kayakers need to be wary of the shoulder dislocation, as do sea kayakers paddling in rough water. Even recreational kayakers paddling in surf zones need to protect themselves from this injury.

Most shoulder dislocations happen because the paddler forgets the three Golden Rules, which we outlined in Chapter 3. In particular, you can put your shoulder at risk by not maintaining a power position. This is usually the result of putting yourself into a situation beyond your comfortable skill level, so the obvious preventative measure is to stick to paddling within your ability and keep practicing the basics, like the three Golden Rules, until they become natural. Another way to help avoid shoulder dislocation is to strengthen the shoulder muscles. Of course, paddling helps to do this, but it's important to note that forward paddling only really works the muscles on the backside of the shoulder. That's why it's important to work back paddling into your warm up. In fact, next time you hit the water, take twenty-five reverse strokes and see how you feel. I'll bet that your shoulders are burning by the end of it—a clear indication that you're using new muscles in new ways.

If you are unfortunate enough to experience a shoulder dislocation, your best option is to get medical attention right away. You can expect your arm to be next to useless, so you will probably want to secure it in the most comfortable position before traveling. If you're in a wilderness setting, far from help, you'll want to reduce (put it back into place) as promptly as possible because the longer is stays dislocated, the more damage can take place in the joint—not to mention the fact that you'll be in considerable pain while the shoulder remains dislocated. With that said, we're going to take a quick look at a technique for reducing an anterior shoulder dislocation. An anterior shoulder dislocation (where the humerus dislocates forward of the joint) is by far the most common of the dislocations (happening over 95 percent of the time). Before going into the details of the technique, please understand and appreciate that I'm not a doctor, so

I can't tell you that this is the absolute best technique. What I can tell you is that it is the technique I learned during a wilderness first aid class and I have used it successfully. Of course, I also learned in the wilderness first aid class that the procedure wasn't guaranteed to work, and that it could potentially do more harm. For this reason, I urge you to use this information as a refresher only. Before you try to reduce a shoulder, take a wilderness first aid course—especially if you're going to travel in areas where you can't get quick medical help.

Assuming you're the rescuer, have the injured person sit, stand or lie down.

Grab hold of the hand of their dislocated shoulder, rotate the arm so that the fingers point skyward and then slowly lift their arm and reach their hand behind their head. Somewhere along the way, the humerus should pop back into the socket and the injured person should experience almost immediate relief. One of the best ways to describe the motion is to imagine a baseball pitcher during the wind-up.

Whether or not you reduce the shoulder dislocation yourself, you really need to seek medical attention right away because damage can very easily have been done during both the dislocating and reducing process.

HYPOTHERMIA

If you're going to be paddling in any type of cold conditions—cold water, cold air temperature or both—you need to be aware of the dangers of hypothermia. Hypothermia occurs when your body is exposed to cold and unable to replenish the heat that it's losing to its surroundings—a condition that can quickly become life threatening unless it's treated.

What makes hypothermia such a real concern for kayakers is the combination of the risk of immersion with the fact that you're often very exposed to weather. For example, your body can cool down extremely quickly if it gets soaked and is then subjected to wind.

Hypothermia has three, recognizably distinct stages—mild, moderate and severe hypothermia. Mild hypothermia involves your body core temperature dropping from its normal 98.6° F, to as low as 96° F. This first stage of hypothermia is indicated by heavy shivering and the inability to do complex motor functions. Moderate hypothermia refers to the condition when your body drops to between 95° and 93° F. At this stage, the shivering will become violent, speech will become slurred and movements slowed, and you will suffer from mild confusion or dazed consciousness. Severe hypothermia results from body temperature dropping between 92° and 86° F, and is immediately life threatening. The body will shut down shivering to conserve energy and virtually all voluntary motor functions will be lost. The body will basically move towards a hibernating condition and awareness will be at a minimum.

The scary thing about hypothermia is that it truly develops as a downward spiral. Once you've crossed the line in which your body cannot replenish the heat it's losing, there's no way to turn the tide without seriously changing the factors playing upon you. We're going to look at those treatments, but first we're going to look at prevention.

In order to understand how to prevent hypothermia, you need to understand the conditions that lead to it. The chief conditions leading to hypothermia are improper clothing for cold temperatures and wetness, fatigue, dehydration and hunger, and alcohol consumption. It should make simple sense that to avoid hypothermia, you need to dress appropriately, travel a reasonable distance, and keep the body fueled with water and food—not alcohol! Pretty simple, really! Problems for kayakers are usually the result of immersion in cold water, or wetness in cold and windy air temperatures. In the Chapter 1 of this book, we talk about the different clothing options for different environments. It's worth mentioning again the fact that there's lots of room for gear in kayaks, so

there's no reason not to bring some extra pieces along. If you need to add some layers while you're on the water, you can raft up with a friend (position your kayaks alongside of each other) and have them hold your boat securely while you make a quick change.

Dehydration is also a major contributor to paddlers' hypothermia, which is ironic when you consider that a kayaker is surrounded with water! One of the biggest causes of dehydration is the inconvenience of needing to go to the bathroom while you're on the water. It's an understandable concern, so you should plan for regular pit stops along the way to make sure you're not afraid to keep drinking water.

Treating mild hypothermia is fairly straightforward. You need to move the person into a sheltered environment protected from wind and stop the loss of heat by removing wet clothing and replacing it with warm, dry clothing. In early stages of hypothermia, keeping physically active is also very helpful for generating body heat. Of course, the body is going to be working hard to reheat itself—and so refueling with water and food is crucial. Depending on the conditions, the body may be past the point of being able to generate more heat than it's losing, so an external source of heat may be needed. This means starting a fire or borrowing someone else's body heat through body-to-body contact. Get the person into dry clothes and then into a sleeping bag next to a non-hypothermic person. If you find yourself dealing with a case of moderate or severe hypothermia, you need to evacuate the person for treatment in a hospital. Until you can get them out of there, you'll want to take whatever measures you can to stop their loss of heat—as described above.

HEAT STROKE

Heat stroke, otherwise referred to as sunstroke and hyperthermia, is basically the opposite of hypothermia. It occurs when the body produces more heat than it can remove—analogous to what happens to a car when it overheats. Heat stroke is a condition quickly worsens, becoming life threatening if not dealt with, so you need to seek immediate medical attention.

The signs for heat stroke are fairly straightforward. Early on, the victim's skin will become red and they will usually experience headaches. They may suffer from dizziness and confusion, and they might faint. As the condition worsens, the skin may actually turn pale or bluish in color and the victim might get the chills, feel nauseous, or suffer convulsions. Obviously, when a person's condition reaches this stage, they're in serious trouble.

The obvious means of preventing heat stroke are to minimize any strenuous activity and to protect yourself from direct sunlight. You also should understand how the body naturally cools itself. The body cools itself (removes heat from the body) through perspiration. The evaporation of sweat provides further cooling. Clearly, the best way to prevent heat stroke is to facilitate the sweating and evaporation processes. That means staying hydrated and wearing loose-fitting, light clothing that maximizes air flow, which helps evaporation. On top of this, it only makes sense to protect yourself from heat-generating factors like the sun.

Treating someone with heat stroke means ensuring they're hydrated and taking steps to cool their body temperature. Get them to drink water, move them into shade and removing excess clothing. You can further help cool them off by bathing them with a wet towel and fanning them to aid in evaporation. You can even immerse them completely in the water, although you need to monitor them closely if you do. Whatever you do to stabilize the person, you need accept the fact that they are done for the day—and likely much longer than that. You need to evacuate them, and get them medical help.

JELLYFISH STINGS

The tentacles of jellyfish contain barbs that adhere to skin and toxins that cause pain and irritation. Tentacles can be free-floating if torn from the jellyfish and are hard to see. Scraping the skin to remove the tentacles is the best response. Use a rigid surface like a credit card or knife edge. Do not rinse the area with freshwater or other liquids, as this simply causes the poison sacs to inject more toxins. Consider taking an antihistamine since there is the risk of an allergic reaction.

STINGRAY STINGS

Sting rays live in shallow water on sandy bottoms—the perfect environment to launch a kayak! Sting rays stick people with a barbed tail when they are trod upon, and you can hardly blame them. Shuffle your feet through the sand and you'll never step on one! If you're unlucky enough to get stuck, your immediate concern will be the phenomenal pain caused by the injected toxin. The toxin isn't dangerous except for the remote chance of an allergic reaction, but the only relief for the pain is to immerse the body part (usually the foot) in very hot water. Take a healthy dose of ibuprofen, but be prepared for about forty-five minutes of agony. Keep refreshing or reheating the water. Not only will hot water help with the pain, but it seems to speed the healing time significantly, too.

GLOSSARY

Assisted rescue
a rescue technique that involves the help of at least one rescuer

Back band / backrest
a padded seat back that provides support for the lower back

Back face
the opposite side of the paddle blade from the power face, used for reverse strokes. Usually convex, with a spine along its center (also non-power face)

Bilge pump
device for pumping water out of a boat

Boat tilt
the balancing of your weight on a single butt cheek or hip, which leans your boat on edge

Body surfing
the position assumed when floating through whitewater: feet downstream, arms out to the side, and the whole body as close to the surface as possible

Bow
the front of a boat

Bow draw
a technique used to turn the boat aggressively by planting the blade near the bow and pulling the bow toward it

Bowline
cord attached to the front of the boat—useful for towing or tying the boat to a dock

Bulkhead
a waterproof wall that divides the interior of a kayak, creating flotation and storage areas, or, an adjustable foot brace system that moves as one unit and lets you apply pressure with most of your foot

Bungee
shock-cords or bungee cords are the elastic lines on the deck of a kayak—perfect for securing gear within easy reach (water bottles, sunscreen, ball cap, etc.)

Capsize
the overturning of a boat so that it goes from being right side up to upside down

Cargo
the items transported in a boat

Chart
a nautical chart is a marine map referencing water features, including depths, shorelines, scale, aids to navigation (like lights and buoys), and other features essential to marine navigation

Coaming
the lip around the cockpit that allows the attachment of a spray skirt

Cockpit
the opening at the center of the kayak

Compass
a magnetic device that indicates magnetic north and the other corresponding points of direction over 360 degrees

Course
the compass direction of travel to a destination

Deck
the top of a kayak

Deck line
rope or shock-cord attached to a
kayak's deck, used for securing
items on deck or to make it easier
to grab the boat

Defensive swimming
passively swimming on your back,
keeping as flat and shallow as possible
with your feet downstream to fend off
obstructions (see also "body surfing")

Downstream
the direction in which the water
is flowing

Drain plug
a stopper, usually mounted in the
stern, that can be removed to drain
a kayak

Draw strokes
dynamic strokes that either pull
water towards or push water away
from the side of the boat at any point
along its length for a variety of effects

Dry bag
a waterproof bag with a seal
(usually a roll-top closing system)
that keeps water out

Dry top
a nylon top with a variety of possible
water resistant coatings and latex
gaskets at the wrists and neck to
keep water out

Ebb tide
the outgoing tide and the resulting
decrease in water depth
(see also "Flood tide")

Eddy
the quiet water behind an obstacle in
current where water flows back in the
opposite direction to the main flow

Eddy line
the point along which the eddy
current and the main current collide

Edging
to tilt your kayak to one side

Face (of a wave)
The part of a wave upstream of the
peak and downstream of the trough
in which water is flowing uphill

Feather
the twist, offset, or difference
in angles between the two blades
of a kayak paddle

Ferry
the technique used to move laterally
across the main current

Float bags
airtight bags that are secured
inside a kayak to displace water
and create flotation

Float plan
an outline of the route and
schedule of a kayak trip

Flood tide
the incoming tide and the resulting increase
in water depth (see also "Ebb tide")

GPS (Global Positioning System) receiver
a battery-powered electronic device that
very accurately calculates positions and
courses based on satellite information

Hatch
the opening into a cargo
compartment in a kayak

High brace
a technique using the front face of
the blade to either recover from a
moment of instability or as support
to help prevent flipping over

Hull
the bottom of a boat

Knot
a measurement of speed—
one nautical mile per hour

Life jacket
a flotation device worn like a vest

Nautical mile
unit of distance used on the sea—
approximately 1.87 kilometers
or 1.15 "land" miles

Paddle float
a flotation device that attaches
to one end of a paddle to create
extra stability

Paddle leash
tether that attaches a paddle
to a kayak

Perimeter lines
cords that run around the edges
of the deck on a kayak, making the
boat easier to grab

PFD—Personal Flotation Device
see "life jacket"

Portage
to carry a kayak or canoe overland

Power face
the side of the paddle blade that
is used for forward strokes

Put-in
the location where you start your trip

Rip cord
the cord at the front of the spray
skirt or spray deck that you pull
to remove the skirt

Riptide
strong current on a beach, created by
waves—potentially very dangerous

Rocker
the curvature of a kayak's hull,
as seen from the side

Rudder
foot-controlled steering mechanism
mounted at the back of a kayak

Scull
the action of moving your paddle
in a way that provides steady and
ongoing power

Scupper
hole that goes through a boat
allowing water to drain off the
deck back into the sea/lake/river

Sea state
surface conditions of the ocean
resulting from winds, swell
and currents

Self-rescue
a rescue technique where the
swimmer reenters their kayak
without aid from a second party

Skeg
a blade or fin that drops into the
water to help a kayak go straight

Spray skirt (also called spray deck)
nylon or neoprene skirt worn around
the waist—attaches to the kayak
coaming to keep water out of the boat

Stern
back of the boat

Stern draw
a technique used to turn or steer the
boat by planting the paddle near the
stern and pulling the boat toward it

Stern pry
a modification of the stern draw, used to steer the boat whereby the back face of the blade is used to pry the stern away from the paddle

Strainer
an obstruction in the river that allows water through, but stops larger objects

Takeout
the location where your paddling trip ends

Thigh hook, or thigh brace
the curved flange in a kayak's coaming that the leg braces against

Throw rope
a rope that gets coiled into a bag, which can be easily thrown from shore to rescue a swimmer in current

Tidal rip
strong current created by changes in tide height

Tide and current tables (also called tide and current atlas)
the collected calculations for tide and current information (times, heights, speeds); organized based on the calendar year, so a recent version is required for accurate information

Tie-down
strap or rope used to secure a kayak to the roof of a vehicle

Torso rotation
winding up the torso to involve major muscle groups in strokes as it unwinds

Tow line
a line that connects a kayak to a rescuer by a quick-release system, typically used to tow a kayak to shore or help an exhausted paddler

Upstream
the direction from which water is flowing

VHF (Very High Frequency)
radio system commonly used in the marine environment; limited to a line-of-sight direct path between the transmitter and the receiver

Wet exit
exiting an upside-down kayak in the water

Wind wave
waves formed by the effects of wind on the surface of water

Whirlpool
a section of downward spiraling current that forms where opposing flows collide

AWARD WINNING OUTDOORS BOOKS AND DVD'S

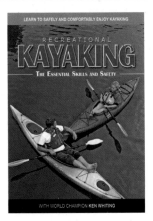

RECREATIONAL KAYAKING

1 Hr, DVD, $19.95

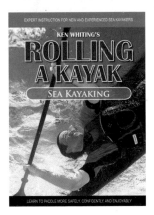

ROLLING A KAYAK

1 Hr, DVD, $26.95

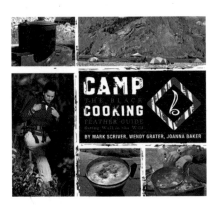

CAMP COOKING

224 pages, Full Color, $19.95

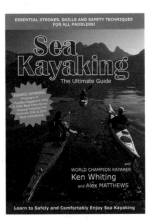

**THE ULTIMATE GUIDE
TO SEA KAYAKING**

2 Hrs, DVD, $29.95

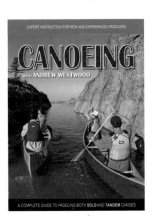

CANOEING

1.5 Hrs, DVD, $19.95

KAYAKING FOR FITNESS

154 pages, Full Color, $19.95

THE **HELICONIA PRESS**